Classroom Close-Ups: 2

Teaching Morality and Religion

Classroom Close-Ups

A series edited by Gerald Haigh which tries to answer the questions 'what really happens?', and 'what really matters?', in education. Titles published are:

'Integrate!' by Gerald Haigh
Teaching Morality and Religion by Alan Harris

and forthcoming books will cover:

Early Reading and Writing
Foundations of Mathematics
Pre-School Education
Games and Physical Education

Other books by Alan Harris

Emergency
Questions about Living
Questions about Sex
Thinking about Education
(with J. Cross) *Language of Ideas*
(with G. Gurney) *Argument*

Classroom Close-Ups: 2

Series Editor: Gerald Haigh

Teaching Morality and Religion

Alan Harris

London   George Allen & Unwin Ltd

Ruskin House   Museum Street

8157

First published in 1976

ISBN 0 04 371029 8 hardback
        0 04 371030 1 paperback

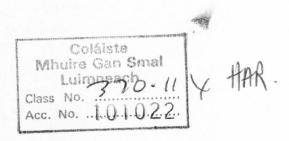

Set in 10 point Press Roman by
Red Lion Setters, Holborn, London
Printed in Great Britain
by Redwood Burn Limited
Trowbridge & Esher

For my sons
Michael and Barnaby

Acknowledgements

Many friends have helped by commenting on the manuscript, but I would particularly like to thank my colleagues David Stringer and Donald Mackinnon. Also my thanks to Pauline Carney, who transformed my scribbles into a manuscript.

Preface

This series of books is intended to offer *practical* help to teachers, and I hope that my own contribution will do just that. However, it is notorious that one cannot separate theory and practice in education, and in this book we are dealing with areas in which most of the practical problems faced by teachers are in fact caused by lack of theoretical understanding. Those who have no clear concept of what 'moral education' means, for example, will obviously have severe practical problems in attempting to provide it.

I make no apologies, therefore, for devoting the earlier chapters to an exploration of what can *count* as being moral and religious education. Only then am I in a position to make suggestions concerning relevant teaching processes.

In order to avoid cluttering the pages with references and footnotes I have often been guilty of presenting borrowed ideas as though they were my own. To put this right I have appended suggestions for further reading, and those who follow up these suggestions will discover the origins of much of my argument. But in particular I am indebted to John Wilson (Department of Education, University of Oxford) and Professor R. M. Hare (Corpus Christi, Oxford): indeed some of my book is no more than a simplification of their own writings.

A.H.

Contents

Introduction

The title of this book will strike some people as being distinctly odd, or even sinister. If I produced a book called *Teaching English and Physics* one would naturally ask why two such distinct subjects should be dealt with between the same covers, and perhaps come to the conclusion that the author had some unusual proposal for integrated or interdisciplinary teaching methods. I wish, therefore, to make it quite clear what the title portends, so that a reader who is totally in disagreement with my premisses need waste no more of his time.

In the first place, I regard moral education as being fundamentally a very different sort of activity from religious education.[1] It has different goals and demands different teaching methods.

In the second place, I certainly do not regard ME as an activity in which teachers of religion necessarily have a special authority (or even a special interest). Moral education is the concern of all parents and all teachers, and it could be argued that the same applies to RE. But there is no reason to suppose that especially gifted teachers in the area of morality should also be gifted RE teachers, or vice versa. Indeed, I would expect, in the average school, that the most effective forms of moral education take place in English lessons and, more haphazardly, in periods defined as 'domestic science', 'health education', 'social studies', and so on. And one of my major concerns in this book is to show how such contributions to moral education can becomes *less* haphazard.

Despite these assertions, however, there are two reasons which led me to adopt the title as it stands.

The first is merely expedient. It does so happen that most RE teachers attempt to provide some sort of moral education, and also that many of their attempts are so grossly misconceived that more harm than good is achieved. If I am right, then it is vitally important that the

---

1. To avoid endless repetition of these terms I shall, reluctantly, sometimes use the abbreviations ME and RE.

kind of works referred to in the bibliography (at the end of this book) should be read by RE teachers.

The second reason is more complex. Although ME and RE are conceptually distinct there are factors they have in common with each other. In particular, they are both areas which involve education of the *emotions*; and therefore an attempt to explore what it *means* to 'educate the emotions' is a necessary prelude to the further study of both topics.

Furthermore, both RE and ME are Cinderellas in the current education system - and, in a way, justly so. In an age when much importance is placed on having very clearly-defined educational 'objectives' those responsible for both ME and RE, in general, fail miserably to compete with mathematicians and scientists in defining what is to count as the successful achievement of relevant, valued goals. It therefore seems appropriate to compare and contrast ways in which such goals could be formulated. We shall find that many of the questions that must be asked apply equally to both topics.

Lastly, a book covering both topics is perhaps justified by the fact that both ME and RE are currently exposed to the same sorts of public criticism. They are 'prescriptive' or 'indoctrinatory'. 'How can anyone *tell* people what is right and wrong?' 'Isn't it hypocritical to *impose* Christian views while pretending to get children to think for themselves?' 'Aren't children inevitably conditioned from birth to hold certain moral and religious attitudes?' I shall hope to show in this book that there are no good reasons for ME and RE, properly conceived, to merit such attacks.

1

Rationality and Emotion

If one states baldly to the average person that part of a teacher's job is to 'educate the emotions' the usual response is one of indignation or hostility. It is accepted that teachers are supposed to foster greater physical or mental skills - and few people would use pejorative terms such as 'manipulate' or 'interfere with' in relation to such activities as teaching people to swim or to do quadratic equations. But the emotions are believed, in a woolly kind of way, to be 'natural' and therefore sacrosanct. It is 'natural' not to be able to read without being taught to do so, but such naturalness is *not* sacrosanct. Emotions, however, are 'spontaneous' or 'uniquely personal' responses to the world, and are somehow 'degraded' if made subject to rational control, or modified as the consequence of conscious introspection.

Yet hardly anyone actually behaves as though emotions were not in some sense educable. Most people accept that one should somehow 'learn' to control one's anger (though they may not be clear about what such 'learning' involves). Few parents would simply accept a small child's fear of the dark as an inescapable fact of emotional life; usually they will, by a combination of reassurance, protectiveness, and reasonableness, help the child to overcome his fear. A girl whose boyfriend is seething with jealousy may wish to end this state of affairs by explaining to him that he is factually mistaken about her relationship with someone else (and therefore that his emotion is inappropriate) or that his jealousy stems from an intrinsically undesirable or unjustifiable possessiveness.

Furthermore, attempts in everyday life to educate the emotions are not simply concerned with the elimination of painful, incapacitating or socially undesirable emotions. In one way or another parents often attempt to foster generosity. Teachers encourage reasoned admiration or respect for works of art and for ways of living. In some cases it makes sense to talk of 'learning to love' someone.

We do not, therefore, actually behave as if emotions must simply be taken for granted. We attempt to influence them in all sorts of ways.

Often we would argue that such influence is *justifiable* on certain grounds. Sometimes we would argue that such influence is *educational*. In later chapters I shall be taking a closer look at processes which, in this context, can properly count as 'educational', and then at the implications of these arguments in the areas of morality and religion. For the moment I shall talk in more general terms.

Let us take one particular emotion - fear - and explore it in greater depth. Here are some instances: an Indian villager is afraid of man-eating lions; a housewife is afraid of mice; an English schoolteacher is afraid of grandfather clocks; an old man is afraid of death; a bank clerk keeps experiencing all the symptoms of fear and yet is not afraid of anything in particular. The example of the bank clerk is not uncommon, but appears to be the most puzzling. Usually fear is characterised by being related to an *object*. If the bank clerk's life is spoiled by continual sensations of fear it would be reasonable to suppose that he would be better off if the physical or psychological causes of these sensations could be discovered and removed by some kind of 'treatment'.

An English schoolteacher is afraid of grandfather clocks.

In the case of the Indian villager, however, it seems entirely appropriate that he is afraid, especially if he already knows of local incidents of other villagers being killed by a lion which is still on the prowl. The most we would say is that he may need to overcome 'blind terror' if he is to survive. There is a difference between being on the one hand 'uncontrollably' afraid and, on the other, being afraid but *doing* something about this particular situation by adopting the best methods of hunting or trapping. And it is clearly often possible to help people to cope with certain natural fears by teaching them how to eliminate or avoid the object of the fear.

'Death' is an 'object' of fear, but not, ultimately, an object which can be eliminated or avoided. Nevertheless, such fear can be more or less reasonable, according to the sort of conscious or unconscious explanation of its cause. Thus if a certain group of people had been led to suppose that death was inevitably followed by an eternity of torment then it would at least be relevant to examine the *basis* of such a belief. Admittedly, fear of death (in our society) tends to be comparatively unformulated, and therefore (rightly or wrongly) less obviously accessible to any external influence.

We are left with the cases of the housewife afraid of mice and the schoolteacher afraid of grandfather clocks. They have in common the fact that generally speaking one would regard such fear as *irrational*. The former case is obviously more common, and is usually to do with unexpected noises, sudden unexpected movements, invasion of order and all sorts of unconscious associations with scurrying, fleeting, archetypal horrors. Normally such a fear, being so common, would not be regarded as necessitating any kind of intervention, 'educational' or otherwise; though an exasperated husband might well futilely repeat that mice are not dangerous.

But the schoolteacher (cited as an instance of those who know what grandfather clocks *are*) presents in our society a different kind of problem. It is a highly complex problem, but it would be generally agreed that since grandfather clocks appear to be an inappropriate object of fear then in some sense it could in some instances be beneficial for the schoolteacher to be brought to the condition of *not* fearing grandfather clocks; and this could possibly involve psycho-therapeutical procedures which arguably involve 're-education'.

I hope that these simple comments (which raise an enormous variety of problems) at least demonstrate one fact. Fear is not an emotion which (like the physical condition of, say, having freckles) is to be viewed simply as an unalterable fact of life. In all cases either the sufferer or the observer (or both) *can* take some kind of desirable action in relation to it; and in some cases such action will amount to a process of education or self-education.

In some sense these remarks apply to all emotions, though we should notice that fear happens to be an example of an emotion which is generally unpleasant and whose effects are *alleviated* by education. True, it may herald an educational process to make small children afraid of electric sockets, or to make the public afraid of the consequences of drunken driving; but education as such would eventually cause the child to *understand* the danger of electric sockets and to avoid sticking a finger into a live one. Understanding would make fear redundant as, in the second example, would universally responsible behaviour on the part of drivers. By contrast, there are some emotions (such as love) which, if directed at appropriate objects, seem intrinsically valuable. Education still has a part to play in relation to such emotions though clearly this is not to make them redundant. This point will be taken up in the next chapter.

For the present let us simply note that already these arguments have very important consequences regarding the nature of moral and religious education. Far from being remote and abstract activities (as many pupils believe them to be on the basis of the way they are taught) such education is concerned intimately with the raw experience of living. All children experience guilt and its opposite (significantly, there is no simple antonym in the English language). All children to some extent experience awe or reverence (though both home and school may inhibit mention of them).

Without wishing to elaborate on such notions as 'starting from the child's own experiences' as a sound educational policy, I can at least uncontroversially state that any attempt at moral or religious education which in no way relates to the actual emotions of pupils is necessarily doomed to failure.

But before developing this theme it is necessary to take a look at the concept of 'education'.

2

Educating the Emotions

Both moral and religious education are bedevilled by the fact that
many of their practitioners fail to recognise what can properly *count*
as education in these fields. Before we move on to some more specific
comments I want therefore to write one more chapter in more general
terms. I hope the reader will bear with me: unless we can agree roughly
on what 'education' means then we will not agree on the natures of
moral and religious education.

Before attempting a definition, I shall continue the arguments of
the last chapters, where I said that there are various ways in which the
emotions can be influenced, but that only some of these ways are
educational. What sort of distinction did I have in mind?

To start with, here are some examples of *non*-educational influences:

1. The emotions can be influenced by the use of drugs or surgery.
For example, a patient is referred to a psychiatrist because he is afraid
of being in confined spaces. This has been a serious nuisance to him,
affecting both his home life and his professional life. The psychiatrist
opts to prescribe the kind of drugs which alleviate the *sensations* of
fear. In this particular case let us suppose that the treatment is
successful in the sense that the patient finds life a good deal more
tolerable. Eventually he is able to manage without using the drugs.

The psychiatrist, then, has certainly influenced the patient's
emotions, but equally certainly he has not *educated* them. The patient
has not learned *why* he experienced 'inappropriate' fear, and if such
fear recurred he would not (as a direct consequence of this treatment)
have either the knowledge or the understanding to cope for himself.
Indeed, the way in which such drugs function is still in some respects
a mystery to the doctors who use them, though of course this is not to
deny the valuable results obtained from these drugs and from equally
puzzling 'treatments' such as electro-convulsive therapy. The use of
drugs is not itself educational, though it may (through rescuing the
patient from overwhelming emotional problems) give him the

opportunity to embark on a self-educational process of intelligent introspection. In some cases (depending on the nature of the causes of the symptoms) such self-education could lead to an end of the problem.

If the administration of drugs is, in itself, no more 'educational' than mending a broken leg, then the same applies to the use of drugs not as 'treatment' but as a means of acquiring new and desired emotional experiences. The states of hallucination, ecstasy, intensified visual perceptions and so on which can result from certain drugs may be experiences from which there is a good deal to learn - but again it is not the taking of the drug which is an educational process.

All the foregoing can perhaps be contrasted with what is supposed to happen during the process of psychoanalysis. As a consequence of intelligent introspection[1] (aided by the analyst) the patient may come to *understand* the causes of his claustrophobia and that fear of confined spaces is an 'irrelevant', 'irrational' outcome. It is not 'really' confined spaces that he is afraid of. If somehow he can learn to come to terms with the real causes of these symptoms then the symptoms themselves may wither away. I do not know if this is a true picture of what psychoanalysts sometimes achieve; but if it is, and if the patient does attain understanding of the *true* causes of his condition, then the process is definitely educational (even if the symptoms persist).

2. There is a famous passage in *Brave New World* where babies just old enough to crawl are shown brightly coloured books and flowers. As they move towards these objects the babies are given electrical shocks. As a result of frequent repetitions of this experience, the babies come to howl in terror at the sight of any books or flowers. This is an example of the process known as *conditioning*. One who is conditioned to have certain responses to an object (whether or not these responses are 'desirable' or not) has certainly not acquired them as a result of an educational process, even if he comes to understand why the response occurs. He was not *taught* to respond in a particular way, and nor did he *learn* to do so in a way which involves the acquisition of knowledge or understanding.

3. Recently, through television, many people have become familiar with propaganda films made by the Nazis. Such films were in themselves instruments of *indoctrination*, and also some of them actually illustrated other techniques of indoctrination used by the Nazis.

1. I do not wish to suggest that any hard and fast distinction exists between methods used by psychiatrists and psychoanalysts. Of course psychiatrists often employ forms of therapy which do not involve 'physical' treatment.

Indoctrination has more in common with education than does
conditioning; for in this case the victim actually does *learn* something,
though what he learns may be false or may be a distorted or partial
version of the truth. It is very difficult to give an adequate definition
of indoctrination, but roughly speaking it is a process by which
someone is led to hold a belief which is not based upon his adequate
knowledge or understanding of the fact upon which such a belief
should rest. Typically, false information is presented in a situation
where the victim is rendered emotionally willing to believe what he is
told. Thus many Germans were led not only to have false beliefs about
Jews (and about the superiority of Aryans) but also to hold such beliefs
passionately. (Note, though, that as a matter of definition people can
also be led to hold true beliefs by a process of indoctrination. The
hallmark is that the beliefs are not 'really' *their* beliefs in the sense that
they are not arrived at by a rational and thorough exercise of their own
minds. The beliefs are, as it were, *implanted* by any technique which
by-passes properly critical exercise of reason.)

4. Lastly, the victims of Nazi indoctrination were often trained to
exterminate Jews. Could we say that they were *educated* to kill Jews,
and if not, why not?

My reasons for rejecting these four processes as educational are
clearly concerned with the constantly recurring words 'knowledge' and
'understanding'. We do not count as educational a process which merely
influences behaviour; it has to be the kind of process which involves
the acquisition of knowledge and understanding of facts and principles.
Furthermore there must perhaps be a sense in which the knowledge and
understanding are *worthwhile*, and this is why we would be reluctant to
say that people can be 'educated' to kill Jews (or, less dramatically,
'educated' in astrology or bingo). Moreover, there is in any case
something odd about 'educating someone *to do something*', for
education is in one respect aimed at making it more possible for people
to choose for themselves what they will do and believe. There is an
important sense in which an educator should as such make himself
redundant, for if those whom he is supposed to be educating remain
dependent on him for further education then he has failed in a crucial
aspect of his task - that of initiating his students into the art of *self*-
education. A mark of the educator (as opposed to the indoctrinator) is
that he will sincerely wish his students to be constructively critical of
what he teaches, that they will be able to correct his mistakes, that
they will overtake him in their knowledge and understanding of his
subject, that they will discover new perspectives and new principles for

themselves, and that the way they *feel* about the world will rationally relate to soundly-acquired *beliefs* about the world.

How many teachers of morality and religion, I wonder, are *educators* in all the senses described above? How many, especially, would find satisfaction if their students forced them to an honest acceptance of the idea that their own moral or religious beliefs were seriously at fault? How many would imagine the mere *possibility* of such a state of affairs?

Some readers may by now feel that I have strayed from my theme for this chapter. I began by talking about the emotions: now I have moved on to what are often defined as *cognitive* objectives (knowledge and understanding) rather than *affective* ones. My argument is that this distinction (popular though it is among modern educational theorists[1]) is fundamentally misleading. For emotions can be more or less rational, and it is only through being concerned with their rationality that educators *as such* have a proper role to play.

If, for example, I have a love of Shakespeare it is simply not good enough to hope that somehow my love will be contagious, will 'rub off' on to my students. Nor, if I respect honesty, will it do merely to 'set an example'. Nor, if I felt reverence for Christ, would it do merely to display this reverence by acts of worship and expect my students to imitate me and thereby somehow to 'catch' the same feeling. If I have good reasons for wanting certain emotional responses to occur then, as an educator, it is with these *reasons* that I am concerned. *Why* do I love Shakespeare? *Why* do I respect honesty? *Why* should a particular object evoke reverence? It is only if I can communicate the rationality of these emotions that I have anything to say as an educator; otherwise at the best my influence will be erratic and at the worst indoctrinatory. By definition it cannot be educational.

Finally, 'affective' education can occur in any subject. In history, for example, certain feelings can be aroused about personalities and events. In maths respect for the elegance of certain proofs can be elicited. But in all subjects 'affective' objectives are not necessarily central, whereas they certainly are in all the Arts, in morality and in religion.

In the remaining chapters, however, I shall confine myself to these last two areas.

---

1. E.g. B. S. Bloom (ed.), *Taxonomy of Educational Objectives* (Longman, 1965).

3

Moral and Religious Emotions

Emotions (as distinct from *moods* such as joy or despair) normally relate to an *object*, are accompanied by physical *sensations*, and provoke some sort of *action*. For example, one may be afraid of a *burglar*, experience sensations such as *trembling*, and be provoked to *hide* or to *summon help*. Education, as we have seen, is concerned with the rationality of emotions and with the rationality of the actions which are provoked.

MORAL EMOTIONS

Among the possible objects of moral emotions are people, actions and abstract ideas. One can respect or despise a man for his character, feel guilt or pride in a particular action, honour truthfulness and courage and loathe deceit or selfishness. Notice that we have a difficulty of vocabulary here, for while words like 'guilt' and 'remorse' occur only in a moral context (it is not appropriate to feel such emotions if one has not done 'wrong') words like 'respect' or 'pride' have all sorts of possible uses. One can respect a man's skill as a fisherman, or take pride in one's appearance, neither of which is a moral issue.

Since I do not have the space to do justice to the richness of our moral language I am going to take an easy way out and talk simply in terms of moral pro-emotions and moral anti-emotions. Furthermore, I shall simplify matters by confining myself in this chapter to moral emotions which have *actions* as their objects (for, as I shall argue later, moral emotions concerning people ultimately relate to what those people *do*, and those concerning abstract ideas, such as justice, again relate to the sort of actions which those ideas entail).

Let us start with a simple example of a moral anti-emotion. A schoolboy finds himself alone in a changing-room. Lying on the floor is an expensive penknife of a type he has always wanted. On impulse he pockets the knife and sets off home with it. However, he begins to feel guilty at so doing. The physical sensations he experiences are difficult to describe - perhaps they could be as strong as trembling, tension, or even nausea (though it is difficult to know whether these simply relate to the element of fear which might be involved). A decision is necessary: he decides not to keep the knife but to hand it in to a teacher.

And now a simple example of a moral pro-emotion. Having broken a window, the boy decides that he ought to own up and offer to pay for the damage. Having done so he feels some pride in the action (something like a warm glow, perhaps) and is disposed to behave in a similar fashion on future occasions.

What interest have these examples to those concerned with moral education? Remember that we are, as educators, concerned with the rationality of the emotion and of the ensuing actions.

In the first case, *why* did the boy feel guilty? Our first impulse is to read more into the situation than may actually be there, and to suppose that the boy felt guilty because he believed stealing to be morally wrong. Furthermore, we may suppose that if pressed the boy would be able to support this belief with an empathic observation such as 'I would be taking away something that the real owner valued, and that's something I wouldn't like to happen to me', or even with a generalisation such as, 'If everyone felt entitled to steal whatever he fancied, society as we know it would cease to exist'. Most people would be inclined to accept these as rational grounds for feeling guilty.

But suppose that his feeling of guilt had a totally different sort of explanation, a fact which we would be likely to discover only if he felt quite differently about other situations in which he was tempted to steal. Suppose, for example, that on his way home from school he stole, without guilt, a transistor radio from a counter in Woolworth's. Or suppose he felt perfectly free to steal from his parents or from foreigners. Or, conversely, suppose, this time just hypothetically, that even if faced with starvation he would not morally countenance stealing food from brutal Nazi invaders - even if he could do so in complete safety. My point is that all we know about the boy from this one instance is that he has experienced a moral anti-emotion to one particular action. It happens to be an action where in our society guilt would be generally thought to be appropriate. What we do *not* know is whether the emotion was *rational* or not, and to educators this is a matter of fundamental importance. As a matter of fact there are all sorts of possible causes of the boy's feeling guilty, and not all of these are causes we would want to call either moral or rational.

For example, he may have heard someone whom he admires (a parent, television personality, soccer star) condemning the idea that 'findings is keepings', and, without asking *why*, he may have internalised this particular rule. Such a response would count as rational only if he had conscious moral reasons for admiring the 'authority' and if he had conscious moral reasons for accepting the rule. There is a wide variety of such pseudo-moral responses, and this will form the subject of a later chapter. For the moment, let us look briefly at some of the educational implications.

*We are much more likely to notice a pupil's moral behaviour
for negative reasons than for positive ones*

In the first place, we are much more likely to notice a pupil's moral behaviour for negative reasons than for positive ones - if, for example, he steals the penknife, or if he is found out to have broken the window without owning up. Too often it is supposed that punishment, accompanied by an exhortation to obey certain rules, is the full extent of the action required. There are all sorts of obvious reasons why such action is inadequate. One is that punishment is certain to be *ineffective* unless the victim *understands why what he has done is regarded as wrong, and can recognise other situations where the same rules would apply*. Another is that while people who understand rules can be trained to obey them there is still the question of *whether the rules themselves are morally good*. Part of the responsibility of the educator is therefore to foster understanding (not necessarily acceptance) of the mores of his society and of the laws and rules which derive from them.

In the second place, schools and parents are much less likely to do anything about moral behaviour which is *acceptable*, despite the fact that such behaviour might well be irrational (or even amoral). It is hardly surprising, therefore, that both parents and teachers are often shocked to discover that children whose behaviour had given no cause for concern start to behave quite differently as soon as they move out of the context of the home or the classroom. Does (and should) the child's apparent respect for property within the home extend to public property such as streetlamps, railway carriage seats and bus shelters? Does (and should) a boy's apparent loyalty and truthfulness to his male friends extend to his first girlfriend and later to his own family? Does (and should) team spirit in school football survive into the factory or office? Does a constructively critical attitude towards school rules

Does (and should) team spirit in school football survive into the factory or office?

develop into a constructively critical attitude to the mores of society as a whole?

My point here is that *ordinary* moral behaviour should be the main object of moral education. It is simply not good enough to regard such education only as 'remedial'.

RELIGIOUS EMOTIONS

Morality and politics are what Aristotle called 'practical' arts. They are concerned with how we actually behave towards each other, and are concerned, at least partly, with making judgements about what is right and wrong. Moral emotions are of great practical importance. Does the same apply to religious emotions such as awe and reverence? And whether or not they have such importance, are they desirable (or otherwise) for their own sake? Can they be more or less rational, like other emotions? There will be a wide variety of reactions to these questions among the readers of this book, partly because to some the question will have an unfamiliar flavour. Yet unless the answer to the last of them is 'yes', then teachers can have no educational role to play in relation to the religious emotions of their pupils. We must first of all, therefore, explore this application of rationality.

One of the many difficulties facing us is that there will be disagreement about what is to *count* as a religious emotion. Presumably there is no difficulty about counting 'love of God', 'reverence for Christ', 'awe of the nature of the Buddha' and so on. But what about being 'in awe of the immensity of the universe', or 'in communion with Nature'? Can one feel awe at the beauty of a flower and call this *religious* awe?

It would, I think, be a serious mistake to adopt too rigid a view of what is to count as a religion, and therefore of the nature of religious emotions. Instead let us see what minimal properties a religion must have, and then be liberal in our interpretation of what particular instances we regard as 'qualifying'. There seem to me to be three such properties:

1. A particular object (or set of objects), which might be a deity, a person, or an abstract idea, inspires a very special sort of emotional response.

2. The emotions inspired include *awe*. This is not a very popular word nowadays, but it is the only one in the English language which specifically characterises such elements as 'feeling extreme reverence for', 'being overwhelmed by', 'feeling very small in comparison with',

'feeling immense wonderment at'. Notice that I have not included 'love' - there are many religions in which this has not been part of the response.
  3. The action which is appropriate to the expression of awe is *worship*, which may or may not become formalised or ritualised. In most religions, however, the element of ritual is a very important one, and is designed to foster, sustain and intensify the worshipper's response to its principal object.

Now if this is a true picture of the essential ingredients of any religion, where does the concept of rationality enter the picture? I suggest that it does so in at least two ways.

  First, is awe an *appropriate* response to the particular object for which it is felt? In the case of *fear*, you will recall, it was suggested that this was an appropriate response to man-eating lions but not (usually) to grandfather clocks, the latter case being irrational in the sense that grandfather clocks are not really dangerous under ordinary conditions. It was also implied that fear would be inappropriate if its imagined object did not in fact exist, or if it did not have any specific object at all. In the case of awe we can apply the same sort of criteria. To do so we shall need to ask if awe is an appropriate response to its particular object (and if its object really exists).

  Second, is worship (or a particular form of worship) an appropriate way of responding to religious emotions? In the case of fear of lions we suggested that running away would be appropriate, but that other alternatives (such as digging traps) may be preferable - and that even *overcoming* the fear might be achieved. So in the case of worship we need to ask what sort of criteria make one form of worship preferable to another, whether any kind of worship is rational, and whether religious awe is an emotion to be valued or to be overcome.

  All these questions we will return to in the chapters on religious education; but since the last few pages have been rather abstract let us just take a quick look at some specific examples of each category.

  First, what makes it appropriate to be in awe of a particular object? Some people might feel this to be an empty question on the grounds that one does not think first and *then* feel awe. Awe just happens: 'it's not a matter of rationality at all'. Well of course it just happens. But what of those who felt awe of Hitler, whose emotions toward him were a combination of veneration, profound respect, reverence and love? And what of Baal-worshippers? Are we to accept that their emotions could not even *conceivably* be altered by some kind of educational process or that (on the principle of everyone to his own taste) no one should be obliged to *justify* the way they feel? It might, of course, prove to be the case that a particular Hitler-worshipper was entirely rational; but it is far more likely that reverence or veneration stemmed from a *false* picture of the sort of person Hitler was - a picture created by a very efficient propaganda machine. If that is true then any educational process which resulted in freedom to see Hitler as he really was would presumably change the learner's emotional response: Hitler would cease to seem an appropriate object of reverence. A different sort of example would be a child who was in awe of a benevolent, bearded anthropomorphic God - a physical entity sitting somewhere just over the clouds. The inappropriateness here stems from the probability that no such entity exists. Eventually the child's concept of God will change, partly as a result of educational processes.

Second, let us look at some examples of the other sort of rational question concerning the appropriateness of worship, or a particular form of worship, as an expression of religious awe. We accept that 'running away' can be a rational response to fear, and that 'going to the theatre' is a rational response to 'love of Shakespeare'. What makes worship a rational activity? And what makes some forms of worship more rational than others?

The first of those questions is mind-boggling, because 'awe' is such a complicated concept. For my own part I would say that often I am in awe of Shakespeare's genius as a poet, or of the immensity of the Milky Way on a clear night; but it does not seem to me remotely appropriate to *worship* Shakespeare, or to fall on my knees and say something like 'O beautiful and immense Milky Way'. Why should religious (rather than aesthetic) awe be different? For the moment, let us accept the simplest answer, which is that just as *looking with special attention at* stars is an appropriate action if one finds them beautiful, so *demonstrating respect for* is an obviously appropriate response to *feeling* reverence, veneration, and so on. Worship is equivalent to such a demonstration.

As for *modes* of worship, it is quite clear that some can be irrational. It would, for example, be strange to worship Christ and to express this by sacrificing human babies in his honour, or to worship the State by praying to it for strength and loyalty, or to worship Buddha by slaughtering all non-Buddhists. These may seem crudely exaggerated instances, but some very strange things have happened in the name of religion. Certainly part of the task of religious education is to promote awareness of this fact.

4

Morality as a 'Subject'

If you, the reader, are in some sense to 'teach morality' to your pupils, it is necessary in the first place to know more about morality than they do. This would not be disputed if the topic were, say, physics or French; one expects teachers to be *authorities* on the subjects they teach, and the higher the level at which they are teaching the more it is essential that they should be thoroughly familiar with the literature of their subjects, and that they should keep up-to-date with new developments.

Is the above paragraph in any way disturbing? If so, perhaps this is because we do not tend to think of 'morality' as a body of knowledge in which (like physics) there are indisputable facts to be transmitted. Moral 'facts' and moral 'rules' are not, it seems, at all like scientific 'facts' or 'laws of nature': people disagree violently about what is right and wrong, and about the criteria on which moral judgements should be based. There are no 'moral authorities' in quite the same sense that there are authorities on Greek literature.

But the differences are more apparent than real. For example, most people would agree that the main job of the science teacher is not to 'transmit facts' but to foster in pupils the ability to think scientifically so that they can become autonomous in their pursuit of scientific knowledge. Similarly the main job of the moral educator is to help pupils to *think morally* so that they can become autonomous moral agents. Furthermore, the status of scientific 'facts' is always open to question. Properly speaking, most scientists would agree, there are no 'facts' - only probabilities. In science one formulates a sensible hypothesis and holds this to be true unless or until it can be disproved. Similarly in morality one can only make hypotheses about what is right and wrong (e.g. matricide is morally wrong) and live according to them until they must be modified by new experience (e.g. matricide may be justifiable under certain exceptional conditions - and then one must appeal to a 'higher order' moral principle such as 'killing one person may be justifiable if the lives of two or more people are thereby

saved'). And finally there *is* a sense in which there are 'moral
authorities' - not people who can tell you what you ought to do but
people who have spent a great deal of time considering the nature of
moral problems and studying the writings of others who have done
the same.

It is an unfortunate fact that most people are not only entirely
ignorant of the work of moral philosophers, but do not see this as
impediment to their role as moral educators. As I have said before, *all*
parents and teachers are sometimes moral educators. If they embarked
on a comparatively trivial task such as learning to repair a television set
they would doubtless have the humility to consult experts on
television, but such humility seldom occurs in the vastly more
important task of moral education.

I cannot, in this book, say anything useful about the *practice* of
moral education until I have first said something about its theoretical
content; and since I have only a few pages in which to do this I hope
that readers unfamiliar with the field of moral philosophy will follow
up some of the suggestions for further reading (see pages 92-94).
Inevitably what I say here about so vast and complex a field will be
little more than a personal view, unsubstantiated by rigorous argument
or by consideration of a variety of alternative approaches.

FREEDOM AND REASON

Morality is that area of behaviour basically concerned with making
judgements about what one ought to do, about what is right and wrong,
good and bad, about duty and obligation. But this is not precise
enough. There are cases where what one ought to do may not be a
moral matter at all (for example, you could say, 'If you want to remove
that stopper you ought to immerse the jar in hot water'). There are
'right' and 'wrong' ways of attempting to solve a jig-saw puzzle, and as
a chauffeur one's 'duties' include driving a car. None of these is
primarily a moral issue, as would be the case if one said 'It is right to
consider other people's feelings', or 'You ought to keep that promise',
or 'It is the duty of all people at the present time to save electricity'.

It is not at all easy to draw a hard and fast line between moral
judgements and other forms of judgement: indeed philosophers
throughout history have debated this issue, and there is still
considerable disagreement among them. However, I shall take the
plunge by agreeing with the following passage by W. K. Frankena:[1]

1. 'The Concept of Morality', *The Journal of Philosophy*, Vol. 63 (1966).

[Morality] includes or consists of judgements (rules, principles, ideals, etc.) that pronounce actions to be right, wrong, good, bad, etc., simply because of the effects they have on the feelings, interests, ideals, etc., of other persons or centers of sentient experience, actual or hypothetical (or perhaps simply because of their effects on humanity, whether in his own person or in that of another). Here 'other' may mean 'some other' or 'all other'.

So far, so good, but perhaps we need to add that moral issues are characterised also by being taken *seriously*. There are obviously matters of *etiquette* which affect other people's interests and feelings, but we regard rules of etiquette as being less important than moral rules or principles. Thus in our own society we may stick to the rule of not publicly belching during a dinner party, but few people would wish to impose this rule in a society where belching is a sign of appreciation of good food. We would generally take a view such as 'it is wrong to hurt people's feelings unnecessarily' and under this moral principle we accept our own rules of etiquette in our own society and different rules elsewhere. The mere act of belching is not in itself a moral issue.

It is not *always* easy to distinguish matters of etiquette from those of morality. For example, in our society at the present time there are many people who would like to be free to sunbathe naked on any beach or in their own garden. What restrains them - etiquette or morality? Doubtless you can yourselves think of many similar examples, and also instances of rules which were once regarded as moral which are now merely matters of etiquette, and vice versa. There is no hard and fast line, but certainly one criterion is the seriousness or importance which we place on certain judgements or rules.

I have already made two large assertions about the nature of morality. It would be as well at this point if you tested them for yourselves: can *you* think of any moral judgement which is neither *(a)* directly concerned with the effects of an action on the feelings, interests, ideals, needs of people or other sentient beings, nor *(b)* to be regarded as in some way important and serious? If not, then you have rejected a large number of ethical theories which have been called *deontological*, i.e. those which place intrinsic value upon moral rules or principles *as such*, irrespective of their consequences in practical terms. Such theories are to be contrasted with teleological accounts of morality, in which rules and principles cannot be evaluated without reference to their intended consequences. Roughly speaking, the contrast between these two classes of theory is illustrated by the rule-dominated moralities of the Old Testament on one hand, and by the rule-as-a-means-to-an-end moralities of the New Testament on the other. In the first instance what makes a person 'good' is his obedience to a fixed set of rules; in the other 'goodness' is characterised by intending to bring about certain consequences. Thus Jesus demonstrated that the intention of helping others could be more important than unthinking obedience to the rule that one must not work on the Sabbath.

We are still a long way from full definition of morality, but before proceeding any further let us look briefly at the educational implications of the last few paragraphs:

1. I have claimed that morality is largely to do with the making of judgements. This in itself is tremendously significant to the teacher. 'Judgements' by their very nature must be made *freely*: I have not made a judgement if I simply repeat what someone else says, or if I repeat words without understanding them (like a parrot), or if I am forced, hypnotised, indoctrinated or conditioned into pronouncing certain words. To make a judgement *I*, nobody else, must freely choose to make it. Furthermore, if it really is a *judgement* that I make, it ought by its very nature be *rational*. One can make irrational *decisions* which might still be good ones, but to *judge* necessarily involves the use of reason.

2. In the case of moral judgements, as we have already seen, their rationality is to do with the intended consequences of actions for the feelings, interests and needs of sentient beings. *Therefore moral education is clearly to do, at least in part, with the promotion of rational thinking, and of knowledge and insight into one's own and others' feelings, interests and needs.*

PRESCRIPTIVITY

Another important characteristic of moral judgements is that as well as being serious they usually *prescribe* a course of action. R. M. Hare[1] puts it this way:

> For if a person is going to reason seriously at all about a moral question, he has to suppose that the moral concepts are going, in his reasoning, to be used prescriptively. One cannot start a moral argument about a certain proposal on the basis that, whatever the conclusion of it, it makes no difference to what anybody is to *do*. When one has arrived at a conclusion, one may then be too weak to put it into practice. But in *arguing* one has to discount this

1. *Freedom and Reason* (OUP, 1973).

possibility; for, as we shall see, to abandon the prescriptivity of one's moral judgements is to unscrew an essential part of the logical mechanism on which such arguments rely. This is why, if a person were to say 'Let's have an argument about this grave moral question which faces us, but let's not think of any conclusion we may come to as requiring anybody to *do* one thing rather than another', we should be likely to accuse him of flippancy, or worse.

Following this line of argument, then, if I say in all seriousness 'I ought to keep this promise' I am not just airing a theoretical point of view, *I am committing myself to a course of action*. My judgement *overrides* other considerations, such as that keeping the promise puts me to some trouble or has other unattractive consequences. By saying 'I ought to keep this promise' I am implying that the obligation (for which, of course, I will have *reasons*) is more important than its side-effects.

If we accept Hare's line of argument then we are abandoning all sorts of moral theories of a descriptive sort. By 'descriptive' I mean any theory which holds a moral word like 'good' to be only a description of actual properties of the object in question. There are all sorts of theories of this kind. For example, some people have held 'good' to describe actions which promote the evolution of man; others have defined it as equivalent to obeying God's will; others believe 'good actions' to be those which promote the greatest possible happiness for the greatest possible number of people; and so on. All these widely different views have in common the fact that 'good' is taken to be equivalent to a set of *facts* about the universe, such that if facts a, b and c apply to a particular action, then that action is good.

I cannot pursue this here except to say that most modern philosophers think that 'descriptive' accounts of goodness are faulty for the following reason. Whereas a word like 'red' or 'circular' simply gives descriptive information about an object, words like 'beautiful' and 'good' seem to function differently. They do not only suggest facts, they *also* function as terms of *approval*.

Some theorists have gone to the other extreme and have said that moral judgements have no descriptive content *at all*. They simply function as expressions of approval, so that if I say 'Jones is a good man' all I really mean is 'I approve of Jones'. Others have held that moral judgements are more akin to commands, so that if I say 'It is good to keep promises' all I am really saying is 'Keep your promises!'

However, such views (though they contain some truth) do not seem to be a *full* account of moral judgements. If I say 'Hitler was an evil man' it does not seem that I am *only* expressing my own disapproval; I am also trying to tell you something about Hitler. And if I say 'You ought to keep promises' the presence of *reasons* of a special sort seem to be indicated, reasons which need not pertain to a straightforward instruction or command such as 'Close the door'.

UNIVERSALISABILITY

But if 'You ought to keep promises' implies more than 'Hurrah for keeping promises' or 'Keep your promises!', what exactly is implied? Many philosophers argue that as well as being prescriptive (like commands) moral judgements must by their logical nature be *universalisable*. Roughly, this means that a judgement such as 'You ought to do x' entails the further judgement that *anyone* in a relevantly similar situation ought to do x.

Suppose, for example, that I am driving towards the brow of a hill and suddenly have to brake hard to avoid a car coming in the opposite direction - a car that had been overtaking a lorry. If I say 'The driver of that car ought not to overtake on the brow of a hill' I must also assent to a universalisation of this judgement, namely that *no one* ought to overtake on the brow of a hill. I cannot use the word 'ought' in a serious moral sense here if I also claim the right to overtake on the brow of a hill whenever *I* want to.

This is not to say that 'overtaking on the brow of a hill' is being taken as a straightforward case of a 'bad' thing to do. Supposing that I were taking a dying child to hospital in the hope of saving his life by obtaining immediate medical care. I *might* claim that the situation justified my taking chances such as overtaking dangerously, but only if I were prepared to universalise this by also agreeing that *anyone in the same situation* would be similarly justified.

Let us take another example, that of the boy tempted to pocket the penknife which he finds in the school changing room. If he thinks morally about the situation he must come to the conclusion either that he has the right to keep the knife or else that he does not have this right. If he makes the former judgement, however, he must also assent to its universalisation: namely that anyone in the same situation would have that right (even if he himself were the owner of the knife and it was someone else who found it). The same thing would apply to the Woolworth's example. If he claims the right to steal then the universalisation is that anyone else has the same right (and since any likely consequences would be unpleasant for society in general he will probably, if he thinks the matter through, decide that after all he cannot really make his original moral judgement).

Since this issue is so important let us take just one further example. A married man is contemplating having an affair with his secretary. If he stops to consider the moral issues, and claims that he *ought* to be able to have such an affair, then morally he ought to accept that anyone in his situation has this right, and furthermore that this should be recognised and accepted as morally justifiable by everyone concerned. Even in his wife's shoes he would have to claim that the husband had the right to have an affair.

Notice that to accept the idea of universalisability does not involve adopting any particular moral creed or viewpoint. In the last example the man is free to accept the universalisation and to go ahead with the affair. He may be quite serious in believing that his wife ought to approve, in which case he is being perfectly consistent.

However, in real life (partly because all humans have a good deal in common, and on the whole share similar interests) the notion of universalisability has formidable consequences if taken seriously. And this is in spite of the fact that it is really only a *logical* account of the nature of moral language, and not a *substantial* moral doctrine such as 'Do by others as you would be done by'.

I am conscious of the fact that in this chapter I have been guilty of gross over-simplifications. As I said at the beginning I do hope that those unfamiliar with the field will follow up the references at their leisure. What I have claimed is too important to be taken on trust.

Meanwhile perhaps you might like to speculate on what the concept of universalisability entails for the following judgements:

'We have the right to own slaves to do all menial tasks for us';

'Women should earn less than men doing the same job';

'I have every right to avoid paying income tax if I can get away with it';

'Children should stay at school till they're eighteen'.

5

The Goals of Moral Education

From what we have said so far about (*a*) the concept of education and
(*b*) the concept of morality, what can uncontroversially be claimed
about the nature of moral education? Let me summarise the main
points:

1. ME, like any other kind of education, cannot consist in *imposing*
a point of view. Education should assist people to become more
autonomous, to make informed judgements of their own.
2. Education does not consist only in imparting facts or rules. Moral
education cannot, therefore, be merely the passing on of information
about the mores of one's own society or those of other societies. A
comparative study of the mores of various social groups is certainly
part of moral education, but ME must go further and foster the ability
to *judge* between various moral beliefs.
3. Moral emotions can be more or less rational. One task of the
educator, therefore, is to help people to decide what particular criteria
are appropriate in judging the rationality of their own moral emotions.
4. These criteria are to do with the effects of one's actions on the
feelings, interests and needs of all people (or all sentient beings)
including oneself. The pupil therefore needs to develop relevant insight
and knowledge.
5. There are no simple, uncontroversial rules about what sort of
results are 'good'. If there were, morality would be comparatively
straightforward. Attempts at simplification (such as 'good actions are
those which promote the interests of the greatest possible number of
people') do not appear to supply infallible guidance in all moral
situations, though often they appear to offer useful guidance in
conjunction with other considerations. Roughly, one might say that in
a particular situation, other things being equal, someone's happiness is
the prime moral target - but in other situations it might be outweighed
by other factors. Moral education must therefore include detailed

consideration of the pros and cons of various 'descriptive' theories of morality.

6. Moral language, specifically the use of words like 'good', 'right' and 'ought', demands close study. Such words are not simply descriptive. In genuinely moral judgements they are usually *prescriptive* and always *universalisable*. The study of the 'logic' of moral language is a very important part of moral education.

All this sounds rather abstract and difficult. Perhaps it seems at this stage that moral education, so conceived, is possible only in the sixth form, with very intelligent pupils. This is not the case. Our arguments so far have practical implications for education at all ages and for all levels of ability.

The aim of moral education is to produce morally educated people. On the basis of the arguments presented so far John Wilson[1] suggests that the essential characteristics of such people are:

1. The attitude that the feelings, needs and interests of other people are equally as important as one's own. Without this attitude one does not even *need* to think morally, for otherwise one could feel perfectly free to use other people as one wished. Nor would one have any real motive for universalising one's judgements.

2. Insight into the needs, feelings and interests of other people (and of oneself) at both a conscious and unconscious level. Without such insight one could not know what hurts people, or is in their interest; and therefore one would lack the basic knowledge which makes rational judgement possible.

3. Sufficient factual knowledge to be able with reasonable success to predict the outcome of one's actions. One might possess characteristics (1) and (2) yet still not achieve a moral goal through sheer ignorance of relevant facts. (One can 'kill a cat through kindness' because of ignorance of what cats need to eat.)

As well as possessing such knowledge, one needs the ability to communicate fluently with as wide a range of people as possible. Unless one has this ability other people, however well disposed, cannot have the opportunity to understand one's feelings and needs; and, conversely, one may never get to the position of understanding theirs.

4. All three characteristics so far defined might be possessed, and yet a particular person faced with a moral decision might not in fact

1. *Moral Thinking* (Heinemann, 1970).

take them into account. He might, for example, *actually* make his decision by such criteria as 'Well, the majority of people would do this', or 'My parents always said I ought to do so-and-so', or 'I'll just obey the law - no one can blame me for doing that'. But the morally educated person will make his *own* judgement, based on (1), (2) and (3).

5. Further, it is essential to be alert and sensitive to situations where a moral judgement is required. (1) to (4) would contribute nothing at all to a person who simply failed to see the need for them to be applied. This is particularly likely to be the case where a situation (however wrong) is so common or is so much a part of a particular culture that it is simply taken for granted. This has been the case - for example with regard to slavery and with regard to an inferior role for women - for the greater part of human history.

6. Lastly, it is essential that one should have the resolution, having made a judgement, to look upon it as both prescriptive and universalisable. One could scarcely regard a person as 'morally educated' if he hardly ever actually *did* what he thought was right, or if he totally failed to apply to himself judgements which he applied to others.

This I personally accept as a comprehensive definition of 'morally educated',[1] and it is apparent, I hope, that all these characteristics *up to a point* can be fostered in any child who is not in some way abnormally handicapped. There is no such thing as the 'completely educated person' in *any* subject, but the greater the degree to which each characteristic can be achieved the more moral education can be regarded as successful.

---

1. But for dissenting views, see suggestions for Further Reading (p. 93).

6

Moral Education in Practice

I want now to distinguish between 'direct' and 'indirect' forms of moral education, and to make some practical suggestions for how both of these can be developed in schools.

By 'direct' moral education I mean a head-on confrontation with problems concerning the very nature and substance of morality. This can take the form of the study of moral language, discussions of the actual moral experience of pupils, and the analysis of real or imaginary moral problems. It is dangerous to be dogmatic about the age at which pupils can cope with what is primarily an intellectual approach to the subject, but what I have in mind will generally apply to children over the age of thirteen. This is not to say, however, that particularly bright and 'verbal' children could not begin much earlier.

By 'indirect' moral education I mean any educational process which could help in the pursuit of our defined objectives, yet which need not *primarily* be intended as moral education. For example, one such objective was a greater insight into people's feelings, needs and interests, and obviously enough there are many aspects of school life which can foster such an insight. The study of literature and the other Arts - creative writing, drama and so on - all contribute to this end.

DIRECT MORAL EDUCATION

I hope it can now be seen that all the chapters so far, though theoretical, *are themselves a practical illustration* of what I would call direct moral education. Of course the technique I have used is suitable only for an adult readership, but the *content* represents a 'course' in moral education which, by the use of different teaching techniques, I have often presented to pupils of average ability in secondary modern schools. Naturally I proceeded at a much more leisurely pace, giving many more examples and illustrations, devising appropriate exercises, and having frequent breaks for open discussion of moral problems posed by the pupils themselves.

There are two main aspects of direct moral education: one is *language-centred*, the other is *problem-centred*. The former seems to me to require a fairly 'formal' approach, building up step by step an understanding of the evaluative and prescriptive uses of language. The latter, too, can be treated in the same way, but should at least be extended and varied with all sorts of discussion, including 'neutrally-chaired' discussions as recommended in the Schools Council Humanities Project.

The language-centred approach
This is illustrated in the next chapter (Case Studies in Moral Education), so I shall say comparatively little about it here. The main point of this approach is to foster much greater sensitivity towards the way in which language functions in moral discourse. I have already explained that some of the major disputes about moral theories are primarily linguistic. It matters very much whether moral words like 'honest' are only 'descriptive' or also 'evaluative' and 'prescriptive'.

Work in this area can begin very simply through the comparison of straightforwardly descriptive words like 'red' and 'circular' with words such as 'frightening' or 'amusing' which give information about the *speaker* as well as about the object being described. If I say that grass is green I am not deliberately giving any significant information about *myself*, but if I say that a certain book is amusing I am saying, among other things, that *I* am amused. Words in this class can also predict the

If I say that grass is green I am not deliberately giving any significant information about myself

reaction of the audience, so that if a drama critic says a play is boring he *can* be predicting that his readers, too, would be bored.

From here one can move on to evaluative words such as 'beautiful', 'elegant', 'honest', 'courageous' and 'good'. Such words not only give varying degrees of 'factual' information about the object itself, but also express an evaluation. It can be shown that not only *characteristically* evaluative words function in this way - practically any word, in a given context, can do so. To say that the Government consists of 'plastic' people would be highly critical, but the word 'plastic' is not, like 'honest', characteristically evaluative.

The next step is to show that while there is usually a clear distinction between statements and commands it is possible for sentences which *look* like statements actually to function as commands. 'The lights are red', spoken to a driver, could effectively mean 'Stop!' This leads on to a close study of the prescriptive nature of many moral judgements. 'That is the right thing to do' can mean much the same as 'You ought to do that', which prescribes a course of action.

Lastly, the notion of universalisability can be explained, with detailed discussion of its implications for a wide variety of moral judgements. This is perhaps the most important aspect of the language-based approach, and requires a good deal of time and imagination.

Expressed in so concentrated a form this may sound a rather difficult and abstract teaching process. In fact, it is nothing of the sort. I can promise you on the evidence of my own experience that average 13 to 16-year-olds are quite able to profit by this sort of linguistic analysis and as a consequence become much more perceptive in their reading of, say, newspaper articles on controversial issues. Indeed, the use of newspaper cuttings for analysis brings topicality and immediacy to the whole process.

Incidentally, there is an important link with RE here. Many of Christ's parables illustrate the need to universalise moral judgements, and every one of the higher religions somewhere or other presents the doctrine 'Do by others as you would be done by'. Brighter pupils can be shown the relationship between this ethical *injunction* and the concept of universalisability as I have described it.[1]

---

1. I have published a course of this kind in books for secondary modern school pupils: Alan Harris and Jack Cross, *The Language of Ideas* (Hutchinson Educational, 1966).

The problem-based approach ♂

Basically this consists of using the criteria of 'morally educated' (as defined in the last chapter) in the discussion of any situation (real or imaginary, fact or fiction) in which a moral judgement has to be made.

Does the person making the judgement really believe that the feelings and needs of other people are equally as important as his own, or does he regard some people (foreigners, the mentally ill, very old people, etc.) as somehow 'not counting' as worthy of equal treatment?

Does he really understand, and have insight into, the feelings and needs of those affected by his judgement?

Does he have enough information about the situation to be able to predict the outcome of his judgement in practical terms for all concerned?

Is he able to communicate fluently with other people about the issues involved?

Does his judgement reflect his own moral principles, or is he abandoning his own principles and judging by some other criteria?

Has he been in the first place able to realise that a judgement was *necessary*, or have things gone wrong simply because he failed to realise this? If he does make a moral judgement, does he have sufficient resolution to *act* upon it and to take seriously its universalisation, or is the spirit willing but the flesh weak?

In practice this battery of questions constitutes a formidable tool of analysis. According to the nature of the situation, of course, some questions will be closer to the heart of the problem than others; but nevertheless here is a good 'routine' for the analysis of almost any moral problem. At this point you might like to take a well-known example from literature of something going wrong morally, and analyse it in the above terms. Consider, for example, the mental process which led up to Macbeth's murder of Duncan. There is every reason to suppose that Macbeth appreciated Duncan's moral rights; he obviously understood Duncan's feelings and needs and knew that he was acting contrary to them (though he had insufficient insight to predict the consequences for his *own* state of mind); and he certainly knew what the factual outcome of his decision would be - Duncan would die and he would become king (though the consequences for other people did not cross his mind). Last, there were no relevant problems of communication in this particular case. What went wrong was that having made the judgement that he ought not to kill Duncan (and this *was* largely his own judgement) he did not have the resolution to *abide* by this judgement. He abandoned morality altogether, and acted purely *expediently* (as he thought).

Doubtless you can think for yourself of contrasting situations in which there was a failure to meet different criteria; and perhaps such examples from literature, being at a distance from the pupils, are a good place to start - especially if the examples are taken from books which they are currently reading. The main point is to habituate them to giving rational consideration to moral problems, and to see and understand the whole range of ways in which moral behaviour can be said to be faulty. But beyond this initial practice it is essential to consider real problems put forward by the pupils themselves so that they come to appreciate the full force of moral thinking in their own lives.

One thing that will come to light is that within the same class (and even within the same pupil) different 'natural' styles of moral thinking will be found to exist, and in relation to these the teacher's job is to foster insight and rational appraisal. Norman Williams[1] has made a fascinating study of these various styles, of the way children are *actually* inclined to make moral judgements; and he classified them as follows. (To illustrate them, I am referring back again to the example of the boy who finds a penknife: if he decides not to keep it, what should he count as a good reason for this decision being the right one? According to his age and personality he might give any one of, or a combination of, these answers.)

1. Amoral Responses
E.g. 'I just didn't feel like taking it.'
The response is egocentric and impulse-guided.

2. Authoritarian Responses   ·
E.g. 'My father says I mustn't keep things I find.'
The response is that the wish or command of some authority is sufficient justification.

3. Conforming Responses
E.g. 'No-one else in my class would have kept it.'
The norms of a particular group or society are sufficient justification.

4. Legalist Responses
E.g. 'It's against the school rules.'
The individual appeals to a generalised and formal authority as the justification.

5. Mass Communication
E.g. 'Val on *Blue Peter* said that findings isn't keepings.'
Statements in newspapers or on the radio or television are used as

1. *Language and Values* (Open University Press, 1973).

sufficient justification.
6. Empathic Responses
E.g. 'The boy who owned the knife could be upset to lose it.'
These are based on criteria to do with the feelings and needs of other people.
7. Theoretical Generalisations
E.g. 'If everyone went around stealing no one's property would be safe.'
These are considerations of what would happen if the judgement were *generally* made.
8. Utilitarian Responses
E.g. 'Society as we know it would be damaged if no one could be safe from thieves.'
In this kind of response, 6 and 7 have been generalised into a kind of rule concerning the interests of society as a whole.
9. Expedient Responses
E.g. 'If I was found out I'd be punished.'
The criteria are concerned with gaining rewards or avoiding punishments.
10. Psychological Expediency
E.g. 'I'd feel guilty if I kept it.'
This is concerned with the avoidance of guilt feelings or the earning of a warm sensation of self-approbation.
11. Social Expediency
E.g. 'My parents would be ashamed of me.'
This is concerned with causing shame in other people or with earning their approval.
12. Irrational Inhibition
E.g. 'It's just wrong, that's all.'
The individual appears to make a clear 'moral' judgement, but no criteria or reasons are supplied.
13. Ego-Ideal
E.g. 'I'm just not the kind of person who would steal.'
The subject refers to some ideal version of himself as a standard of comparison.

In this theoretical analysis we find yet again a *practical* tool for moral education, for it is a fairly easy task to devise a set of 'moral situations' and, for each one, to list examples of each of the possible types of response. One can then discuss these responses with the class, first of all eliciting from them which response they would favour themselves, and then as a group considering the merit of their choice.

For it is not difficult to see in the light of our previous arguments that only a few styles of response are 'moral' in the full sense of the term. Number 6, the 'empathic response', is within our moral framework because morality is to do with the effects of behaviour on others (but note that one could have insight into others and use this insight for one's own selfish ends - nevertheless moral responses should, among other things, be empathic). Number 7, 'theoretical generalisations', and number 8, 'utilitarian responses', are also within our framework; for rationality in regard to consequences is involved, and here we have the beginnings of the universalisation of moral judgements. However, it is not until universalisability as we have defined it becomes a conscious part of judgement that the judgement becomes moral in the full sense.

By contrast, the other responses are pre-moral or amoral if considered as *sufficient* justification. For example Number 2, the 'authoritarian response', is inadequate unless the individual has moral reasons for accepting the authority in question, and Number 3, the 'conforming response', is inadequate because the characteristic judgements of the group may be morally at fault.

Analytic discussion of all these issues should in itself do much to educate the moral emotions of the group. Always the move towards rationality will begin from a consideration of the individual's own feelings and judgements.

Norman Williams goes on to fit these various responses into a matrix where two broad classifications are used. On one hand, some responses he calls 'thinking' (where the individual primarily has regard for the consequences of an action) and some he calls 'referring' (where the responsibility for judgement is passed on elsewhere); on the other hand he distinguishes between 'self-related' responses (where the agent is concerned primarily with consequences for himself) and 'other-related' responses (where he is concerned with the consequences for others).

	THINKING	REFERRING
SELF-RELATED	(1)	(3)
OTHER RELATED	(2)	(4)

In this matrix (1) represents responses which are both 'thinking' and 'self-related' (such as *expedient* responses), (2) consists of 'thinking' and 'other related' responses (such as *empathic*), (3) consists of 'self-related' and 'referring' responses (such as *ego-ideal* or *irrational inhibition*) and (4) consists of 'other-related' and 'referring' responses (such as *authoritarian, conforming* and *legalist*). The responses of any individual tend to fall within one or other of these classifications, which may be called his *preferred mode of moral response*. Generally speaking, the more mature a person becomes the more likely it is that his preferred mode will be (2), and certainly a rough measure of the success of moral education would be a movement from other modes towards (2) - but only if mode (2) is preferred on *rational* grounds.

Finally, a word about class discussions in general. It is well known that the discussion technique is full of pitfalls for the unwary. Some of them are as follows:

1. In a class of thirty or more each pupil could only speak for a minute or so in one lesson. What is the guarantee that those who are not speaking are profitably involved in the discussion?

2. Most teachers talk too much and mistakenly believe that they are always making their pupils think for themselves. Too few teachers are able to avoid the mere (superficial) imposition of their own views.

3. Usually two or three pupils monopolise the discussion.

4. On delicate moral issues (especially those involving sex) pupils may be reluctant to expose pressing moral problems, and discussion can therefore remain artificial and superficial.

There is no altogether satisfactory solution to these problems, but here are some suggestions. In the first place it is a waste of time for a teacher to get involved at all if he is not on close, trusted terms with his pupils - better then to stay with formal methods. Second, even if you do not accept the arguments underlying the Humanities Project it is excellent practice to have occasional discussions in which your own role is strictly neutral in that you discreetly keep things going without ever giving your own views and without giving an overt reaction to those of the pupils. Third, it is a good idea (if the geography of the school permits) to split the class into groups of half a dozen, arrange for there to be a chairman in each one, allow the groups to conduct their discussions in private, and simply to ask for a chairman's report on the conclusions drawn. I am not pretending that this is an easy procedure - many factors make it difficult - but if relationships between class and teacher are good then this is probably the most effective form of learning by discussion.

In order to help with the early stages of initiating a class into this procedure I wrote a book called *Questions about Living*[1] which

1. Hutchinson, 1968.

contains structured questions on fifty controversial issues. Pupils in small groups can use this book until they feel competent to do without this kind of help.

INDIRECT MORAL EDUCATION

So far I have talked about direct confrontation with moral problems, and have suggested methods applicable to children of 13+ in lessons labelled either 'English', 'social studies', or even 'ME'. But what of younger children, and what of the other sorts of contribution the school can make? I shall now take each of John Wilson's components and indicate briefly what educational processes are relevant.

1. *The attitude that the feelings, needs and interests of other people are equally as important as one's own.*
One cannot *make* people care about others or regard them as equals. If one is deficient in these respects it is probably because of the nature of one's early family relationships, and what schools can do about this is very limited indeed. However, the attitude is at least likely to be fostered in a democratic environment where pupils are encouraged to work with each other rather than to compete, where work is organised on a collaborative project-type basis, where pupils meet others from widely different social backgrounds, where there is a good deal of informal contact between staff and pupils, and where pupils are encouraged to do work which brings them into contact with all sorts of people in the outside world.

The attitude in question can vary in *extent* and in *intensity*. We cannot do very much about the intensity with which one person cares about others; but there is more to be said about cases where someone regards some people as equal but not others. Suppose, for example, that a particular person regards Negroes as inferior, or thinks that the Chinese are shifty and cunning, or that the mentally ill do not have the same moral rights as others. Usually this is an unthinking attitude, or one based on positively mistaken ideas about the group in question: the more one has contact with a group the less likely one is in practice to regard its members as outside the scope of ordinary moral thinking.

I cannot dwell on the educational implications here; they are obvious enough. But let me give just one example. Many teenagers have sexual relationships without bothering to use contraception. In part this may be because they do not think of babies as human beings with the same rights as anyone else, so it does not occur to them that they are risking potentially serious deprivation for an unwanted baby. I think that it would make *some* contribution to the solution of this problem if *all* teenagers (especially boys, perhaps) took a course in child care which brought them into actual contact with infants from birth to the age of five or six. This would work no magic, but at least it would foster awareness of the fact that babies have feelings and needs that must be taken into account.

It would foster awareness of the fact that babies have feelings and needs that must be taken into account

2. *Insight into the feelings and needs of other people and into one's own feelings and needs.*

Much said under (1) applies here too. The organisation of the school and curriculum can help or hinder the kind of relationships which foster insight. Nine-year-olds sitting in rows facing the formal teacher will learn less in this respect than children working in small flexible groups.

Most important, however, is the role of literature and the other Arts.

Self-knowledge is fostered by well-conceived encouragement in the areas of creative writing and improvised drama, and, obviously, by the sympathetic study of novels, poetry and plays. I cannot enlarge upon this because a separate book would be needed.

A plea for innovation, though. Why on earth should we devote so much time to, say, maths or botany and none at all to psychology and philosophy? For if there are two subjects which are transparently of central importance for all people, these are the ones. It is the greatest priority in all secondary schools to develop suitable courses for pupils of all levels of ability. It is nonsense to suppose that philosophy is too 'difficult' for the average child. All children philosophise every day of their lives, and processes can be devised to help them do it *better*.

3. *Sufficient factual knowledge to be able to predict the outcome of one's actions.*

In the context of morality this means, especially, knowledge of the *mores* of one's own and other societies, for unless one understands various systems of moral rules, laws and principles (understanding does not necessarily imply *acceptance*) it is impossible to understand moral behaviour in those societies and therefore impossible to predict the effects of one's *own* behaviour. What we have here then, is a subject called 'comparative morality' which is just as essential an ingredient of moral education as 'comparative religion' is of RE. In a conventional timetable one would hope that the enlightened teaching of geography, social studies, and literature would all contribute to this end (though I grimly remember that when at school myself I spent five years studying North and South America without gaining any knowledge whatsoever of what it was like to *live* there).

4. *The ability to communicate fluently, so that there is maximum mutual understanding.*

The relevance of various aspects of English teaching is obvious here; I need not enlarge upon them except to say that traditional grammar schools have been very much at fault in neglecting oracy.

Less obviously relevant is enlightened physical education (including dance). The English are notoriously bad at using the expressive capacities of their bodies. Again, the nature of relationships within the school is highly important. Any curriculum which fosters close pupil/pupil and pupil/teacher relationships will promote communicative skills.

5. *The ability to form one's own principles of behaviour.*

I have dealt extensively with this item in the first half of this chapter under the heading of 'Direct Moral Education'. This ability will emerge with practice in the rational discussion of moral issues.

6. *Sensitivity towards the need for moral judgements, and resolution
   in putting these judgements into practice.*

Sensitivity should be fostered by many of the techniques already
discussed. Resolution is a tougher problem. How can one make people
resolute?

I have two suggestions. One is that self-confidence can be developed if
adults take seriously what pupils produce in the way of moral judgements, and help them to think clearly about them. It is no good

*This would be folly of the same order as encouraging 'personal writing'
and then tearing up the results*

encouraging children to make their own judgements if these are greeted
with contempt, frivolity or tight-lipped disapproval; this would be folly
of the same order as encouraging 'personal writing' and then tearing up
the results.

This leads to the second suggestion. Pupils need *practice* in making
judgements and in facing up to the consequences of them. Therefore

within the context of the school every attempt should be made to give pupils genuine responsibility both concerning their own work and concerning the running of the school. By this I do not mean merely a school council which is allowed to make suggestions that can be vetoed by the staff; I mean *real*, if limited, power. Only in this way do pupils genuinely have to face the consequences of their own decisions.

7

Case Studies in Moral Education

As illustrations of moral education in progress I include here
illustrations of language-based and problem-based methods. The first
consists simply of an extract from materials which I have used with
pupils in the early stages of the study of moral language. The reader
may like to consider how he would use this material with his own
pupils. The second is an entirely imaginary, but not untypical, example
of a classroom discussion of moral problems. The third is based on my
own experience in secondary modern schools.

LANGUAGE-BASED METHODS[1]

You may have been taught in English Grammar that most adjectives
are words which name qualities of objects. When a person says,
'Grass is green', or 'That man is honest', you assume that 'greenness'
is a quality of the grass and that 'honesty' is a quality of the man,
and that the speaker's intention is to draw this quality to your
attention.

In fact, it is worth thinking about three quite different sorts of
work that adjectives of quality can do. Only one of them is purely
descriptive, as when you say a hoop is 'circular' or glass is
'transparent'. The other two are more complicated.

Adjectives can indicate that an object has certain properties
which are likely to arouse certain emotions. Just by saying that a
view is 'sublime' you give no factual information about the view
except to suggest that it must have certain (unspecified) qualities
which are likely to arouse a certain sort of emotion in most people.
If you say a vase is 'beautiful' you are not giving factual information
as you would be if you said it was 'earthenware'. You are suggesting
that it has certain (unspecified) properties likely to arouse a certain

---

1. From *The Language of Ideas*, Book 2, by Alan Harris and Jack Cross
(Hutchinson Educational, 1966).

sort of feeling. By saying an experience was 'terrifying' you are not giving factual information as you would by saying the experience was 'brief'. You suggest that other people, had they shared the same experience, would have found the same adjectives appropriate.

The third use of adjectives is to suggest that an object has a certain moral quality. If you say that an action is 'praiseworthy' or 'damnable' you mean that other people too should find that action morally good or bad. Here are some further examples of the three uses:

(*a*)   A man may be blue-eyed, amusing and admirable.

      'Blue-eyed' is simply descriptive.

      'Amusing' suggests that other people (but not *all* other people) will also find him amusing.

      'Admirable' suggests that he has certain moral qualities which are morally desirable.

(*b*)   A dress may be red, comfortable and indecent.

      'Red' is simply descriptive. (No ordinary person would dispute this fact, though a colour-blind person would have to take another person's word for it.)

      'Comfortable' suggests that some other people would also find a similar type of dress comfortable, if it were designed to fit them.

      'Indecent' suggests that other people, as well as the speaker, should find the dress objectionable on moral grounds.

(*c*)   A ball in cricket may be a leg-break, tempting, over-pitched.

      'Leg-break' is simply descriptive. If the ball turns in a certain direction described by 'leg-break' then there can be no argument about this.

      'Tempting' suggests that other batsmen would also share the experience of wanting to hit it for six.

      'Over-pitched' suggests a *judgment*. This time it is not a *moral* judgment, but nevertheless a judgment on which experienced cricketers would expect to agree. To hold an *opinion* like 'This ball is over-pitched' is not the same as to have *feeling* such as 'I'd love to hit this for six!'

Sometimes a word can have hidden implications. To call a dandelion a 'weed' is at first sight merely to describe it. But what do we *mean* by calling it a weed? If we are looking at plants just for pleasure and say that a dandelion is a weed, we mean that it is an unwanted plant, and we would expect other people to share the same feeling about it. But a *professional* gardener, by calling a dandelion a weed, may mean that it *ought* to be removed.

Points to Consider

1. Comment on the use of the following italicised adjectives. Are they (*a*) merely descriptive, or (*b*) do they suggest that other people would have a certain sort of feeling, or (*c*) do they suggest that a *moral* attitude is demanded? Or are they (*b*) *and* (*c*)?

The chair is *comfortable*.
This is an *enjoyable* book.
That is a *deplorable* error.
Ebony is *hard*.
It was a *disappointing* match.
What *disgusting* behaviour!
This is a *manufactured* article.
She was wearing *ridiculous* clothes.
The castle was *secure* against the enemy.
The smell is *unbearable*.
The scarf is *perfumed*.
America is a *decadent* country.
He is a *vicious* criminal.
His behaviour is *perfect*.
What a *funny* face he has.
He acted with *commendable* speed.
They had a *hair-raising* escape from death.
Here is a *wooden* bowl.
He had a *wooden* expression.
He was unforgivably *rude*.

2. In paragraph 3 what 'unspecified' qualities might make a view 'sublime'? What 'unspecified' qualities might make a vase 'beautiful'?
3. 'Over-pitched' is a judgment word when applied to a ball in cricket. What judgment words can describe handwriting, a road surface, wallpaper, a screw-driver, glue?
4. When you describe a person as being sincere, generous, honest or reliable, are you also saying that you *approve* of this trait? Or would it make sense to say, 'He is a very generous person, so I disapprove of him'? When you describe a person as mean, cowardly or selfish, do you also imply that you *disapprove* of this trait? Would it make sense to say, 'He is a coward, and I admire him for that'?
5. You would not say that a film was 'amusing' unless you expected other people to find it so. Would you expect everyone to find it amusing if you did? Would you expect the majority of people, or just a few people to find it amusing?
6. If a person is honest, would you expect everyone to agree that

this was a good quality in him? Or the majority of people? Or just a few people?

Further Work
Make notes on the kind of work done by each adjective in any one page of a novel.
Make lists of 25 words expressing moral approval and 25 expressing moral disapproval.
What work is done by the word 'ugly' in:

(*a*) an ugly face
(*b*) an ugly customer
(*c*) an ugly bruise
(*d*) an ugly moment
(*e*) an ugly smile

PROBLEM-BASED METHODS (1)

Class 4B filed into the classroom very quietly. Their English teacher, Mr Belfry, was a strict disciplinarian and they did not wish to be kept in after school - the date being 5 November.

Mr Belfry cast an eye over them as they came in. 'Don't *slouch*, Parfitt. Meadows, go away and put on your school tie. You look *naked*, boy.'

When they had settled down the teacher stood squarely in front of them, his thumbs hooked portentously behind his lapels. He paused theatrically. 'Today', he boomed, '*I'm* not going to teach *you*. *You're* going to teach *me*. *SIT UP, SMITH*. We're going to have a discussion, and this time *you* lot are going to do the work. Now then, *THINK*. Who can suggest any topic at all where different people in the class would have different points of view? Something you could all really get your teeth into, and have a real old argument.'

4B were only used to answering questions when they knew what the right answer was supposed to be. This time there was no clue, and therefore silence.

'Come on, there must be *something* that interests you. Or', he added ominously, 'shall we carry on with punctuation?'

A sense of urgency suddenly pervaded the classroom. Fiona Higgins put up her hand.

'Sir, is abortion ever, sort of, *right*?'

'No. Abortion is *NOT*, sort of, right. Any *sensible* suggestions?'

4B racked their brains. What on earth did he want them to discuss?

Finch, the form captain, tried. 'Should we discuss the dispute between the miners and the Government, sir?'

'Better, better. But does anyone here know the *facts*? Would you know what you were talking about, or would you just *waffle*? Try again.'

Meadows tried his luck - taking a big risk. 'Sir, could we discuss whether or not there should be a school uniform?'

'Aha', said Mr Belfry. 'A subtle hint from the naked ape. Very well, let's hear the views of the class. Should there be compulsory school uniform, or should you be allowed to wear filthy leather jackets or transparent lace trouser suits?'

'Sir, I think there should be a uniform because otherwise less well-off children would get shown up. They couldn't afford what others could.' (That was the form creep.)

'Good, good. Now is there any answer to *that*?'

'It wouldn't be so bad, sir,' said Fiona, 'only why can't the pupils have some say in what the uniform should be?'

'A budding Mary Quant, I see. Who can give me three reasons why pupils are the last people on earth who should have any say in the matter? *You*, Jones. You haven't spoken yet. Give me three reasons.'

Jones miserably racked his brain to no avail.

'Come on boy, this is a *discussion*. Contribute.'

The form creep came to the rescue again. 'We don't know about the costs of mass production or anything, sir.'

'Good, good. And you don't know anything about design, and anyway most of you have the most appalling taste in clothes. Now then, who can think of any sensible arguments *against* uniform. Let's be fair and look at both sides of the case.'

'It stamps out individuality,' suggested a girl who was known to have skin transfers of the Osmonds in rather naughty places.

'*SIR*,' barked Mr Belfry.

'It stamps out individuality, sir.'

'Well it's *SUPPOSED* to stamp out individuality, you silly girl, so that teachers aren't encouraged to have favourites because some children are decently dressed and others are long-haired scruffs. Now has anyone any *sensible* arguments?'

There was a very long pause.

'All right, then. It's quite apparent that you aren't in the least interested in having a pleasant change from routine. Get out your grammar books.'

With a gentle sigh of relief, 4B turned to Chapter 6, 'How to avoid the word "got".'

'and anyway most of you have the most appalling taste in clothes'

PROBLEM-BASED METHODS (2)

It is easy enough to make fun of Mr Belfry, but not so easy to put better pedagogical ideas into practice. I have already mentioned some of the difficulties of conducting class discussions, and will end this section with a description of an approach that I have tried out myself in secondary modern schools.

First, though, a few words about the Schools Council Humanities Curriculum Project. Most of you will be familiar with Stenhouse's basic ideas. His team produced packages of materials on such themes as war, sexual relationships, the family and so on, each of which includes press cuttings, poems, photographs, short stories, tapes of songs, etc. Each package is intended to provide ample 'evidence' which could be used for discussion of various aspects of the central theme. This evidence is supposed to be 'neutral' in the sense that the various items are not collated in a way intended to present a false, biased or partial picture of the theme. Stenhouse's advice on the use of this material is that:

1. pupils should be in a comparatively informal setting, e.g. they should be sitting round a table rather than in rows of desks;
2. the teacher should act as a 'neutral chairman', helping pupils to locate 'evidence' of immediate relevance to the discussion in progress but *not* giving any points of view of his own and *not* indicating any favourable or unfavourable response to any point of view expressed by a pupil.

The main point of all this is to achieve a democratic situation in which pupils will actively learn to form views of their own about fundamentally important issues, rather than passively accept instruction from the teacher.

This brief outline of the project does not do justice to Stenhouse's educational theories, and I therefore hope that readers unfamiliar with the materials will find out more about them. However, it is clear enough from what I have said that the educational process involved is poles apart from Mr Belfry's approach.

1. The setting is informal and relaxed.
2. The posture of the teacher is not authoritarian.
3. Pupils are genuinely free to pursue topics which interest them.
4. The outcome (in terms of how their attitudes change, what they learn, and what skills they develop) is unpredictable.
5. The pupils do nearly all the talking.

My own attitude to the Stenhouse experiment is that it provides a much-needed corrective to bad authoritarian teaching. Even if one does not accept all Stenhouse's arguments it is a valuable and chastening experience to play the role of the neutral chairman; the odds are that, like most teachers, one has always been inclined to talk a good deal too much oneself, and has not tried hard enough to leave the real work to the pupils.

On the other hand, I hope that the neutrally chaired discussion does not, as an educational device, encourage teachers to abandon their role as *academic* 'authorities'. Though such discussions are valuable (much as, by analogy, it is valuable for pupils to play a real football match interrupted only by ordinary refereeing) their value is immeasurably enhanced if pupils are also formally learning the skills and knowledge which make conversation *worthwhile* (just as they need to do exercises of various sorts in order to make the game of soccer more worthwhile). With regard to conversations in which moral issues are being discussed there are, for example, rules of logic which need to be taken into account; and, even more importantly, there are rational considerations about the nature of morality (as I have expounded at some length) which need to be studied formally. Otherwise, pupils tend to make little progress beyond merely exchanging points of view. It is very hard work to think clearly about moral issues, and it is pointless to pretend otherwise.

My own experiments in secondary modern schools were closer to Stenhouse than to Belfry, but included the elements of 'direct' moral education described on pages 40-48. As for 'discussion periods' I sometimes adopted the technique of dividing the class into groups of five or six, each of which had one member who acted as chairman and one who recorded the main outcomes of the discussion.

The starting point was simply a controversial statement of the sort which would predictably lead to a range of different opinions being expressed. For this purpose I borrowed the entire 'attitude inventory' from Michael Schofield's book[1] which included statements on a very wide range of topics such as:

Each person should decide for himself what is right and wrong;
The family should spend an evening at home together at least once a week;
Young people should be taught all about birth control;
The average man can live a good life without religion.

1.   *The Sexual Behaviour of Young People* (Penguin, 1970).

There are a hundred statements of this sort in the inventory, and I decided to use these statements in particular because the process of Schofield's research had produced a very accurate picture of how teenagers throughout the country responded to them. Thus I was able to show the pupils (at some stage) a block graph indicating the proportion of boys and girls who agreed or disagreed, strongly or mildly, with each statement; and thus the pupils could compare their own views with those of the majority.

It seemed unlikely that the pupils would, without previous practice in group work of this sort, be able to organise discussions of sustained relevance to the basic theme, to incorporate a sufficiently wide range of points of view, or to know at all times what sort of evidence would be relevant in supporting their arguments. I therefore printed each statement on a separate card together with a battery of questions and (where appropriate) some relevant factual information. The pupils were free to ignore all this if they wished (and, ultimately, were encouraged to do so); but in the early stages they found the structured questions quite helpful. Here, as an example, are extracts from one such card:

If a boy gets a girl pregnant he should be willing to marry her

Questions to help your discussion

If the couple had intended to get married in any case, they will probably get married as quickly as possible. But supposing they didn't intend to? Is it right for them to get married if they aren't in love with each other?

   Which of these factors are the most important?

(*a*)   Children need a father.
(*b*)   Forced marriages are much more likely to end in divorce, which is probably even more harmful to children than early adoption.
(*c*)   The girl's reputation will suffer if she's not married.
(*d*)   An illegitimate child may suffer later when he discovers the fact for the first time.
(*e*)   A boy forced to marry against his wishes may be a resentful, discontented husband.
(*f*)   No parents can disguise from children their feelings towards one another.

   At what age can a girl get married? What is meant by 'the age of consent'? At what age can a girl get married without the permission of her parents?

   Suppose a girl of seventeen gets pregnant, and wants to

---

marry the boy. Her parents forbid the marriage. Is there any way in which she could legally go ahead?

Do you think it is wrong for a boy to have intercourse if he would not be entirely willing to marry the girl?

Some facts to consider

The replies of 158 younger girls and 241 older girls to the question: What would you do if you were going to have a baby?

	Younger girls, %	Older girls, %
Tell parents	42	35
Try to marry the father	16	24
Make arrangements to keep it	16	20
Try to have it adopted	8	9
Get rid of it	8	6
Other	3	2
Don't know/couldn't happen	7	4
TOTAL	100	100
No. (100%)	158	241

Why do *fewer* of the older girls say they will tell their parents? Isn't it obvious that they will have to tell them? Only a quarter of the older girls *say* they would try to marry the father, but do you think that many more would try if the situation actually occurred?

A *third* of the boys said they would be willing to marry their girlfriend if she became pregnant.

Deliberate abortion (when the baby is removed from the womb while it is still very tiny) is only legal in special circumstances. Except when done by a skilled doctor under hospital conditions it is also *very dangerous*. Find out why this is so.

What other teenagers think

If a boy gets a girl pregnant he should be willing to marry her.

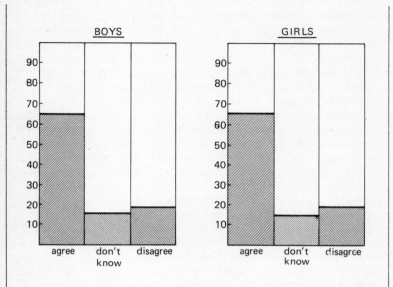

BOYS   GIRLS

agree   don't   disagree   agree   don't   disagree
         know   know

One third of the boys said they would be willing to marry their girlfriend in the event of her becoming pregnant. Why do *more* than a third agree with the statement under discussion?

On the whole, I feel that this experiment was successful as one step in the process of moral education. It had its faults in that (despite the considerable choice of topic available) pupils were being directed into a process which is best if it happens spontaneously in relation to a topic of immediate concern. However, seen as a sort of trial run in the right direction the work did, I think, ultimately facilitate higher standards of thought and argument when these *did* arise naturally from the context of the pupils' own lives.

As compared with the Stenhouse materials my work cards (if only because of their brevity) were sometimes 'loaded' towards a vaguely liberal point of view. However, in due course, when the pupils were familiar with several of the cards, this fact was one that we were able to discuss as an issue in itself. Some of the pupils even had a go at producing cards for other classes to use and had intensive debates among themselves about the existence or otherwise of bias in their own materials.

Theoretically, then, I think the experiment was reasonably sound. In practical terms there were problems I never entirely solved.

If one has five discussion groups in the same classroom the level of sound, however considerate each group tries to be, is not conducive to the clearest of thinking. If one spreads groups around the school (on the playing-field, in the dining-room, and so on) even the most reliable of pupils are likely to get distracted. If, however, one can lay one's hands on two or three portable cassette tape-recorders this can eliminate some of the problems. If absent groups have to record the whole of their discussion then the length of the play-back should coincide with the length of the group's absence from the classroom, and could be used to check on how each member of the group contributed to the discussion. Thus the mere presence of the microphone provides a pressure to concentrate on the work in hand. In any case, the tapes come in useful when different groups compare their treatment of the same theme: in one school we had a budding radio producer who was very adept at editing various tapes in such a way as to bring together the most significant passages into one half-hour programme, and this provided the starting point for a round-up of the moral and logical issues arising from the original theme.

Lastly, there is the problem of how to form the various groups. If one started in the first place with a large mixed-ability group of, say, thirty-five pupils, should each of the discussion groups also be as mixed as possible? Or is there anything to be gained by highly verbal children forming a homogeneous group? Or should the groups be designed all to include reliable pupils who will temper the behaviour of the less reliable ones? These are questions, of course, which are central to all the debates about the nature of comprehensive education. My own unspectacular conclusion is that pupils should decide for themselves how they split up; and, if one wishes as a teacher to modify such groups, it is desirable to give reasons for doing so. These reasons could well form the basis of yet another discussion!

8

Religion as a Subject

What does it mean to 'teach religion'? Teaching *about* religion seems
an easier concept: there is the *history* of religions; the *sociology* of
religions; the *comparative study* of religious beliefs and practices; the
aesthetic study of religious texts, music and art; and the *psychology* of
religious belief and behaviour. All these are respectable academic
pursuits, and all of them have some part to play in RE.

Yet, if we seek a parallel with 'teaching morality', none of them
seems to strike to the heart of the matter, just as we would not be
content *only* with the history of moral codes, the sociology of moral
behaviour, the comparative study of diverse moral codes, the literary
study of writings about morality, or the psychological study of moral
growth and attitudes. But at least we can accept all these as *educational*
processes, and as such to be contrasted with *indoctrination*, 'bringing
children up to be Christians', and so on.

What is missing from this impressive list? Perhaps the clue lies in our
argument that moral education aims at helping people to 'think
morally', thereby becoming, as far as possible, autonomous moral
agents. Furthermore, ME is partly concerned with the language of
morality, the logic of its key concepts, the problem of establishing the
'truth' of moral judgements: in short, the whole problem of *thinking
clearly* about morality. What parallels should we expect to find in RE?

This question is perhaps not so appallingly difficult as it may at first
seem; but only if we are willing to step back for a while from our own
beliefs and to search dispassionately for the answers we need. The
trouble is that while many people in our society are used to the idea
that one can argue rationally about moral issues the same does not
apply to religion. We live in a complex society with a wide range of
cultural heritages, and we have grown accustomed to constructive
scepticism, and to the need to resolve the conflict between different
styles of moral thinking. But this does not apply to religion: very few
people have got beyond the stage of saying 'Oh well, everyone to his
own beliefs' (with the hidden assumption that in any case it does not

matter very much what religious beliefs anyone has). It is as though, morally, we were still at the tribal stage of taking for granted the notion that our own mores are unchallengeably 'right' and that foreigners were just 'different' or 'inferior' or eccentric. This is hardly surprising, for most of us are brought up in a way which precludes thinking objectively (or even thinking at all) about religion.

Stepping back from our beliefs (or non-beliefs) takes a concentrated effort of imagination, however; so I am going to adopt the device of *inventing* a religion in order that we can see what educational questions would be involved.

Imagine a primitive agricultural society cut off from the rest of the world. It is widely believed that the sun has human characteristics - a mind and will of its own, and the power to manipulate events on the earth. What the sun actually does can be influenced by prayer, but only prayer conducted by virgin males who have never tasted food that grows below the ground (such as root vegetables) or in areas of permanent shade. The sun god is wantonly cruel to mankind, but receives the souls of the virgin male priests provided that their bodies are burned at noon. It is not believed that any other people apart from the priests have souls, and therefore only the priests need education (in order to prepare for absorption into the body of the sun god - which always takes place at the age of 25, when they are bound and cast on to a pyre). Other people simply learn the basics of agriculture, housewifery and war (for the sun god decrees the death of any strangers who penetrate the country).

The main questions to be asked are obvious enough:

1. Why is the sun thought to have human characteristics? How is the sun supposed to communicate?

2. Given that it really had these characteristics, is it a suitable object for awe (as opposed to enforced respect or wonder)? Is worship an appropriate response (as opposed to expedient obedience)?

3. Is the *nature* of worship rational - why should it matter whether or not this is conducted by virgin males, and what is the relevance of their diet?

4. One of the central beliefs is that there is, for priests, an afterlife which involves becoming part of the sun. But what does this mean? Is some kind of personal identity retained? Is the afterlife of a desirable nature?

5. What generally is the effect of this religion on the quality of life? What does the religion offer to compensate for the enforced ignorance of the majority and the sacrifice of the young priests? What is gained from killing strangers?

6. What attitude should outsiders take? 'Well, that's their religion and they're entitled to it', or 'It would be right to impose some other religion upon them, first by force and then by indoctrination', or 'It would be right to find some way of getting these people to question their own beliefs, perhaps by giving them alternative possibilities to think about'? Or what?

I have deliberately invented a silly religion with the express purpose of showing that religions *can* be silly. Part of the nature of religious education (not accomplished by comprative studies as such) is to expose *all* religion to the light of reason so that people are free to decide for themselves whether, say, Christianity has more to offer a critically enquiring mind. But let us now be more systematic. In relation to any religion, RE can raise the following issues:

1. What is the main object, or what are the main objects, of awe, reverence, veneration and so on? If this is some form of Being which has a will, (*a*) on what grounds is such a Being believed to exist, and are these convincing grounds; and (*b*) do awe, reverence and so on seem appropriate responses to the Being in question, and by what criteria can this be judged? If the object is not a Being with human characteristics such as a will, an interest in human beings and so on (if, say, it is an abstract concept such as love) can awe and reverence *possibly* be appropriate responses? If the Being is a human being, dead or alive, what singles it out as an appropriate object of awe as compared with other human beings?

2. Is any actual form of worship particularly appropriate or inappropriate to the object in question? Are other religious activities, such as prayer, *rational* activities, and if so, by what criteria? For example, why should fasting, or other forms of sacrifice, be appropriate? Could one have reasonable beliefs about the object, but unreasonable ones about worship, and vice versa?

3. What other religious beliefs (apart from those concerning the existence and nature of the object) pertain to a particular religion? What is their derivation? Are they consistent with each other?

4. As far as one can tell, what are the effects of a particular religion on the general quality of life of the believers? How would these effects be judged by other criteria, such as those of morality and aesthetics? If they are thought to be good are they patently a result of the religious beliefs rather than of other human qualities? If they are thought to be bad, is this because in some sense the religion itself is bad, or because over a period of time the religion has lost its original power and is being distorted or misunderstood by its followers? For example, is what I

would call the appalling abuse of women and girls in some Roman Catholic and Muslim countries a necessary consequence of those religions or is it really inconsistent with them?

I am afraid that these questions are over-simplified almost to the point of being naive. I have framed them in an attempt to formulate the basis of an investigation into *any* religion, and therefore they are very general (though, as I see it, fundamental). Naturally the study of any particular religion would make it necessary to pursue some questions rather than others in depth. Nevertheless, viewed dispassionately, they would all seem to be questions that need to be asked.

By this point many readers may be hostile to my emphasis on rationality. Surely, it will be argued, religion is not a matter of reason: it is a matter of faith, therefore any attempt to consider religion purely in the light of reason is completely missing the point of what religion is all about.

There is some justice in this line of thought, but it needs several qualifications. For even if one accepts that religion is a matter of faith (whatever that means) it still makes sense to ask whether or not that faith is rational (or desirable in any other way). If someone assured me, as a matter of faith, that my living-room was full of invisible and inaudible singing pigs, then I would not regard his use of the word 'faith' as exempting him from the need for some kind of educational influence (which, for all I know, may give him more *communicable* reasons for believing in the pigs).

It may still be argued, however, that although religious propositions such as 'There is an omnipotent, benevolent God' have the form of propositions such as 'There is a place called London', they do not really function in the same way at all. Rather, they mean something like the following: 'I have feelings about the universe which can only be expressed through figures of speech. I do not mean, *literally*, that there is a physical entity with these characteristics (indeed, if there *were* this would be more a matter of science than religion), but that I find it helpful, in facing the imponderable complexity of the universe, to think, act and feel *as though* there really were such a being.'

Now if this sort of approach is taken to be the 'meaning' of religious statements then it is clearly a waste of time[1] to deal with them as though they were scientific statements. They are simply not (and not intended to be) verifiable in the same way. It is often very helpful to say things like 'I feel as though there's a great weight pressing on my mind' even though it would clearly be a ridiculous response to look for the actual weight. But even if this attitude is taken, the other questions I presented can still be asked, specifically that concerning the effects of religion on the quality of life.

In particular, this involves us with the need to 'get the feel' of a religion, to 'see it from the inside'. For we cannot with any complete scientific accuracy judge that a certain religion does in fact have specific consequences for our way of life. It is too easy, if we have faith, to attribute the good consequences to the religion and the bad ones to misunderstanding or distortion of the religion (indeed the literature of most religions is full of ingenious attempts at doing just this!). All we can do is attempt an enormous imaginative leap to try to experience *what it is like* wholeheartedly to belong to a particular faith. The feelings which we then have are just as subject to rational

1. However, even if religious discourse is taken to be *metaphorical*, there are still criteria of a rational sort which can be applied to the appropriateness (and helpfulness) of the metaphors involved. One simply moves towards the criteria used in aesthetic criticism.

evaluation as the feelings we have when, say, listening to music. For it does make perfectly good sense to say things like: 'When I first heard that piece I found it overwhelmingly impressive, but now that I have more experience of music I find it rather banal and sugary. And this is not just because my taste has changed - I know I have *better* taste than I used to.' By analogy one could say that while reading 'Genesis' one found God pretty impressive, but that after reading the rest of the Bible one looks back to a rather petulant figure, not at all deserving of reverence. And in the same way one can compare religions of quite different origins.

I shall argue in the next chapter that the most important task in RE is to help pupils make the sort of imaginative leap that I described above, and to make it in relation to a variety of religions. But beyond this they should be helped to evaluate critically the experiences so gained.

9

Religious Education in Practice

It is impossible to understand much of history, much of art, many of the conflicts in contemporary society and the contrasting life-styles of different ethnic groups in our own country without having some understanding of various religions. For these reasons alone it seems ridiculous that there should be disputes about the existence of RE as part of the normal syllabus of all schools.

Such disputes usually arise because RE is supposed to be inevitably indoctrinatory and to involve pupils in activities in which they should have the right not to participate. There are good grounds for this supposition; I have yet to see a school where RE was not flagrantly indoctrinatory, though I have heard of several which are more enlightened (and these include several Roman Catholic schools). But the same thing often applies to the teaching of history, literature and many other subjects. This is not a case for abandoning teaching in these areas (or there would be precious little left on the syllabus) but of finding better teaching methods.

As with ME, I want first to distinguish between 'direct' and 'indirect' religious education. 'Direct RE' I shall take to be concerned with a head-on confrontation with the meaning of religious concepts, with the language used in religious discourse, and with specifically religious beliefs and activities. By 'indirect RE' I shall mean the organising of experience by which pupils may come to a better understanding of various religions.

DIRECT RELIGIOUS EDUCATION

People have always felt that there are important questions about the nature of the universe which cannot be answered by scientific, mathematical or philosophical methods: 'Who made the universe?'; 'What is the purpose of life?'; 'Are men machines, or do they have souls?'; and so on.

Those who ask such questions are not usually satisfied with the kind of answers provided by philosophers. One can say, 'But the question "Who made the universe?" presupposes that it *was* made, and that it was made by a purposeful being. Why should one presuppose this, and how in any case could such a being be *outside* the universe?' Or in response to 'What is the purpose of life?' one can say 'Objects like chairs have a purpose because they were *made* for a purpose. Why should one suppose that a purposeful being created life? - and anyway such a being would already have been an instance of "life".' And so on. But while it is easy enough to demonstrate that all these are 'non-questions' (in the sense that no answer would possibly satisfy the questioner - he simply does not know what kind of answer he wants) the questions go on being asked.

With older pupils I take the first task of direct RE to be a general consideration of the 'big' religious questions, and of the criteria by which they might be answered. This will involve a comparison with other 'forms of thought' such as science, history, mathematics, art and philosophy, all of which pose different sorts of questions and which have their own distinct methodologies and criteria for verification. It should emerge from this kind of enquiry that there have always been muddles caused by people treating questions in one category as though they belonged to another: for example it has often been wrongly supposed that the question 'is there a god who created life?' is by its nature *scientific*, and can be verified or falsified by empirical procedures. Yet few people have stopped to think what would emerge if scientists said: 'Yes, there *is* a sentient being in the fifth dimension which causally affects our lives'. It would still need to be asked: 'But is this being a *god*?' And such a question could not be answered by scientists, because there are no scientific criteria of 'godliness'.

So what sort of questions *are* religious ones? Are they all non-questions, as has been argued by the logical positivists? Are they simply devoid of meaning because they contain terms like 'God' and 'soul' which denote nothing in the 'real' world? Or are they to be seen as metaphorical, as a way of expressing otherwise indefinable, but significant and important, questions about the nature of the universe?

It will be realised that there is a massive disagreement among theologians about this issue, even among those who profess the same religion. One only has to remember all the Roman Catholic debates about the nature of hell, or more recently the heart-searching of John Robinson in *Honest to God*, or, in America, the evolution of the 'God is dead' sort of 'theology'. It would therefore be quite wrong for any teacher to present only one point of view, and I am quite sure that average children of thirteen upwards are perfectly capable (if taught well) of appreciating at least in essence the point of the current arguments.

However, there are serious implications for the education of RE teachers, many of whom tend to be limited in their knowledge and skill to a simple form of Bible study and a homely form of pastoral care. In order for pupils really to get to grips with religious language and to be able to think for themselves it is essential that RE teachers should have a hard intellectual grasp of modern theology and of the philosophy of religion, otherwise they had best not to pretend to offer RE at all (as opposed to other important but carefully circumscribed tasks such as education in the *history* of religion, and so on).

If this sounds a harsh judgement, it is meant to be. Whether one is dealing with undergraduates, sixthformers or with John Smith in 2D there is no professional excuse for ignorance of the subject one is supposed to be teaching. The alternative is realistic and simple, and that is not to teach it at all.

INDIRECT RELIGIOUS EDUCATION

As in the case of morality, I think that this most effectively begins with the experiences of the pupils themselves. What sort of religious experiences have *they* had, as opposed to experiences which have arbitrarily been imposed upon them?

It seems likely that there will be a parallel with their moral development as explored by psychologists (notably Piaget and Kohlberg). Roughly, this is said to consist of a 'pre-moral' stage, an authoritarian stage ('what my parents tell me to do is "right"'), a conforming stage ('the norms of my peer group are "right"'), and lastly an 'autonomous' stage, in which young people come to make their own moral judgements on the basis of some sort of generalised principles.

This can apply to religion in two ways. The first is simple. Children will first accept what their parents and teachers say about religion, then they will tend to conform to the attitudes of their peer group, and lastly they will begin to think for themselves. But there is a more important and complex analogy. The 'authoritarian' stage is that at which any concept of a god is closely related to that of all-knowing and all-powerful parents. Later, probably during adolescence, young people's religious feelings are likely to be generated within the culture of a small group of peers where, in what might be called a quasi-religious sort of way, certain 'cult figures' (who might be film stars, pop singers or whatever) become objects of 'worship'. In this context certain ideals are formed (tough heroism, romantic love, wanton destructiveness), and certain rituals (even forms of 'uniform') are established. And in the final stage (which may never be reached) there is a conscious re-direction of these religious feelings - a voluntary commitment, perhaps, to some form of Christianity, or to Zen Buddhism, or to communism or humanism.

The bulk of pupils in secondary schools will be at the 'conforming', or 'cult', stage. This can take an enormous variety of forms. It seems to me that here the main task of the teacher is to discuss with pupils the nature of all those quasi-religious experiences with which they will be familiar. What is the real nature of the cult figures? What sort of ideals are being pursued and what sort of values are inherent in, say, romantic love? What forms does the quasi-worship of the cult figures take (such as hysteria at pop festivals, freak-outs for Jesus Christ Superstar, the fetishism of sex-worship)? What is the overall effect on the life style of those concerned? How is this effect to be evaluated?

If the teacher is really sensitive towards, and open-minded about, these teenage cults (many of which, of course, may have the *appearance* of being more orthodoxly religious) a number of valuable educational results may be achieved. For one thing, the average 'agnostic' will discover to his surprise that his beliefs and behaviour do in fact have something in common with those of 'religious' people. He is almost certain to have faith in something and/or somebody, a faith which goes beyond any rational justification that he could give for it. He will see that, like other worshippers, he has rituals which he never thought of as being in any way religious. He has beliefs which it has never occurred to him to question.

All this should at the very least enable him to come to a better understanding of the nature of formal religions, and at best should lead him to a rational appraisal of his peer group's cult figures, faith, behaviour and beliefs. These he should learn to compare and contrast with those of other social groups, in his own country and elsewhere.

The stage is now set for his development towards autonomy. Conceivably the insights already gained will lead him in some sense to abandon religion altogether: he may come to see it as a phase of growth (an important one) during which the individual (and indeed mankind as a whole) needs to 'explain' the vast and hostile universe in which he finds himself, and to be able in a small way (perhaps through prayer) to *influence* the unimaginable forces that it contains. In other words he may come to think that even the most sophisticated of religions has in common with sun-worship the fact that it was invented by men as a way of satisfying powerful psychological needs, that in fact men are protecting their sanity by *falsifying* the nature of the universe.

On the other hand, he may well find that RE brings back to life for him the religion in which he was 'brought up' and against which he had reacted as an ordinary part of adolescent rebellion. Perhaps his first conscious experiences of, say, Christianity were unfortunate ones in that he was indoctrinated with simplistic or distorted views of Christian beliefs, in which case RE may not only bring him a more accurate picture but could also give him valuable insights into his growth as a person.

This is the stage, in any case, at which it seems appropriate that the bulk of RE should consist of a comparative study of major religions and of quasi-religions such as communism, Nazism and (possibly) existentialism. I doubt if much impact could be made by RE lessons *alone*, however. Integration between many subjects - history, literature, social studies, music, art (and, hopefully, psychology and philosophy!) - is essential if anything approaching adequate understanding is to be achieved. 'Direct RE' can, as I suggested, deal with some of the basic concepts of the religions, and this is very important. But it is even more important that pupils 'get the feel' of various religions, 'see them from the inside', and get to know what it is *like* to have a particular religious philosophy. And this cannot possibly be achieved by one discipline alone.

To get the feel of Nazism, for example, pupils would need to know of the inter-war economic factors which swept Hitler into power, and to know of the political factors which gave credibility and popularity to his nationalism. They would need to understand the racial tensions, the general mood of the working classes, the frustrations heaped upon the ordinary German people consequent on the first world war. Even more important, to have some concept of Hitler's charisma, they would need to see films of the Nuremberg rallies and Nazi propaganda films, and perhaps even dramatise for themselves key incidents in the Nazi regime.

All this is not simply learning *about* religion. Background knowledge is essential, but the main point here is ultimately to get to grips with religion as a way of thinking and feeling.

With regard to the various forms of Christianity, these are, of course, more accessible to the majority of people in this country. It should not be too difficult for pupils to gain understanding, say, of the contrast between Roman Catholicism and Quakerism in terms of fundamental beliefs, attitudes, religious practices and life styles - provided again that there is integration between all relevant subjects.

The kind of thing that will emerge from comparative study is that all religions have an important role to play in helping people to come to terms with the inevitable frustrations of life. We have wants and needs, but many of them (inherently) cannot be satisfied, and in any case our wants and needs often conflict with each other. The various religions offer different 'philosophies of life' which help their followers to reconcile themselves to these difficulties - and all of them do so in different ways, by offering different styles of solution. An understanding of these various 'styles' is perhaps the most effective way 'into' a religion.

Buddhism, for example, solves the problem of frustrated desires by decreeing the *abandonment* of these desires. In order to attain Nirvana, the merging of the soul with the cosmos, it is necessary to put aside all desires and all forms of egocentricity. (This negation of self is also to be found in some quasi-religions, including communism, where the self becomes absorbed, as it were, into the State - though here the 'feel' of the religion is radically different.) Buddhism clearly has much in common with other Eastern religions such as Confucianism or Taoism.

As a 'style' of answer to life's problems, Buddhism has quasi-religious relations with many attitudes to life which we find in the West, so it is not surprising that many young Americans are (literally) taking a 'trip' to the East. Their baffled reaction to a world with which they cannot cope is to resort to complete passivism, or to escape through the use of drugs, or to vague attempts at imitating the much more disciplined forms of meditation to be found in the East.

By complete contrast, Epicureanism advocated the pursuit of pleasure (though not necessary *trivial* pleasure by any means, nor even entirely 'selfish' pleasure); life is hard, but we only have one life - let us weather the storm and find enjoyment where we can. This, too, clearly has resonances in our own society.

Again by contrast, the philosophy of the Stoics was that life is grim and hard, but must be suffered with dignity and courage. We must retain our identity, but at the cost of considerable pain. This too is an ideal which is reflected in our own culture and in the States. Many cult figures in films and television plays are men who take all the punishment that life can mete out, but who retain their own battered integrity.

Christianity (at least in some of its forms) seems to be an amalgam of several philosophies, though the overriding one is the philosophy of love, integration and brotherhood. Sometimes, though, *selfless* love is emphasised - a 'surrendering' of oneself to God, the abandonment of personal desires, service to others - and here elements of Buddhism seem to be echoed, though with what some people would argue to be a more positive sort of motivation. Sometimes there are elements of Stoicism (suffer, be true to yourself - but there is a reward in Heaven). Sometimes there is emphasis on the pleasure and joy of life (given the right relationships with God and Man); sometimes there is a grim emphasis on self-sacrifice and purifying pain. Sometimes materialistic attitudes are sanctioned, at others the emphasis is on the spiritual dangers of wealth and property.

It is impossible to give a prescription for how schools can most effectively foster insights of this sort - the dangers of trivialisation and over-simplification are obvious. Certainly the enterprise must be inter-disciplinary. Certain religious texts (simplified if necessary) should be used. Certainly the life styles should be brought home by actual contact with different religious communities (where this is possible), by the use of films, literature, drama and so on. But all this depends on the talents of particular teachers and the resources of particular schools.

What is of overriding importance is that pupils should not simply be presented with variety, as on a supermarket shelf, but should bring some critical understanding to bear. I hope that this chapter has at least indicated some possible lines of approach.

10

Case Studies in Religious Education

In this chapter I present three examples of RE in action, the first of which is fictitious but based on a real incident.

1. EXPERIMENT IN A PRIMARY SCHOOL

Miss Gifkins, in her final teaching practice before qualifying as a teacher, was assigned to a tiny Church of England village school which basically consisted of two classrooms, one for the infants and one for the twenty children aged from seven to eleven. Her main subject was mathematics, but of course in this situation she had to try her hand at everything including the statutory RE.

The headmistress said that the juniors were 'doing missionaries', and that Miss Gifkins must continue the good work. And so, in her first week, she sometimes had the task of conducting morning service with the aid of a book called *Praise the Lord* (Book 4) and then of confronting twenty suitably chastened pupils with stories (from a book printed in the heyday of the British Empire) about how kindly, bearded patriarchs brought enlightenment to the grateful Africans.

Miss Gifkins was troubled. Apart from the fact that she had difficulty in communicating with the whole age range from seven to eleven by means of such formal methods, she was also aware that her formidable tutor, an atheist who insisted on students calling him by his Christian name (Karl), was unlikely to be impressed by her achievements. Her worst suspicions were confirmed when he arrived at one of her rare moments of desperation - she happened to be beating a bored seven-year-old over the head with a rolled-up wall chart of the saints and shrieking: 'What does "civilisation" *mean*, child?'

'My God', he said. 'How can you teach such drivel?'

'But I have to do missionaries', she pleaded.

'Right. We'll *do* missionaries. But not this way.'

He proceeded to explain that junior school children could hardly be expected to identify with either Victorian missionaries or with their grateful hosts. 'Take the *concept* of "missionary" and translate it into modern idiom,' he suggested. 'How about door-to-door encyclopedia salesmen?'

'Or', suggested Miss Gifkins, 'how about the first missionary to Mars? Lots of art-work, costumes, drama?'

'Great', said Karl.

'But supposing the vicar turned up', said Miss Gifkins. 'He's always likely to appear before morning coffee.'

'Great', said Karl. 'Invite him to play the part of the missionary.'

And so it transpired one day that the vicar, wearing motor-cycling gear and carrying a goldfish bowl under his arm, strode into the classroom with the words: 'I come in peace, in the name of the Father, the Son and the Holy Ghost.'

He was confronted by twenty children ingeniously diguised as intelligent lizards.

'Hello', said one. 'Why have your brought your fish?'

Miss Gifkins nudged a well-rehearsed lizard. 'We believe in the Red Rain God', it said. 'He brings oxygen to our crops, and kills the Sand Serpent. What do *you* believe in? Would you like a cup of tea?'

'Yes, please', said the vicar. 'I believe in one God, all-powerful, who made Man and Martian. No sugar, thank you.'

'Where does your God live?'

'God lives inside us all. He is everywhere.'

'But where's his head? Does he have a funny head like yours, or a proper one like ours?'

'Think of God, if you like, as having a head like yours. Anyway, he sent his son Jesus to save us all . . .'

'Why didn't Jesus come to Mars?'

'Well he couldn't go everywhere, could he? So he arranged for people like me to come instead, to tell you about God.'

'But if God's already inside us why did he need to send you? Why doesn't he just say hello himself?'

The lizards wriggled their tails excitedly - too excitedly, for at this point a huge papier mâché model of the Sand Serpent was rocked off the top of the cupboard and fell into the vicar's lap.

Later, Miss Gifkins felt that on the whole the experiment had been a success, at least in terms of the drama and art work. And long after her departure from the village the local farmers were successfully following their children's advice on how to invoke rain.

2. AN INTERDISCIPLINARY APPROACH

Miss Gifkin's lesson had, in conception, a good deal to recommend it, despite her own reservations. It was an imaginative idea to put the pupils in a position where they were called upon to see Christianity 'from the outside', as something strange and alien. In principle this is a device which facilitates clear critical thinking and a fresh emotional contact, though of course Miss Gifkin's pupils were too young to gain much benefit in intellectual terms even if the lesson had gone according to plan. As you will see, this 'distancing' of the pupils from familiar ideas is a feature also of the following experiment which was conducted in a comprehensive school with pupils of fourteen upwards.

The starting point was a school production of Marlowe's *Dr Faustus*. All too often 'the school play' can be a pretentious waste of time, aimed more at impressing the outside world than with catering for the educational needs of the pupils. There must be hundreds of schools in which, during rehearsal time, many classes are left to kick their heels while the few pupils actively engaged in the production take over the school hall and the attention of a dozen or so of the staff. (And usually, of course, it is the A-streamers who perform and the C-streamers who are expected to do menial tasks such as putting out the chairs.)

On this occasion, however, every pupil in the upper school was involved in one way or another, and it was the work of the art department which sparked off a plan for interdisciplinary study occupying nearly a whole term.

What do devils *look* like? What sort of costumes would be needed for the creatures who ultimately drag Faustus down to hell? Should there be some sort of glimpse of hell at the end, and if so should it be a smoky sulphurous cavern, or what? According to Mephistopheles, Faustus was in hell even while on earth ('Why, this is hell, nor are we out of it'), so why the need for fire and brimstone? Why *down* to hell?

The inclination of the art teacher was to create devils of the sort depicted by Hieronymus Bosch, and to have Faustus dragged into a cavern mouth from which smoke billowed; but the producer (head of the English department) suggested that a group of sixth formers did some research into what sort of expectations an Elizabethan audience would have had. At the same time it was decided to re-create, as far as possible, the sort of performance which would originally have been given.

When the fourth and fifth formers became involved in making costumes and props and in constructing the stage, there began many arguments among them about the existence of heaven and hell, and about the existence of gods and devils. The atmosphere was one in which it seemed appropriate for the teachers involved in the play to pick up some of these issues in class.

In art, English literature and music, pupils were introduced (roughly in chronological sequence) to various ways in which heaven and hell have been depicted. In RE, pupils learned something about pre-Christian and non-Christian views on the subject, and about changing images and beliefs throughout the history of Christianity. This involved a look at the different ways in which God is personified throughout the Bible, at various beliefs about the nature of the soul and life after death, at the impact of scientific thinking, at the concept of divine justice and so on.

In English lessons the moral issues were debated: what is 'free will', what is the justice of eternal damnation, and how do concepts of justice relate to concepts of freedom, fatalism, determinism and so on?

In science, time was found (despite the examination syllabus) to consider (if only superficially) psychological 'explanations' of religious beliefs. Freud's views were considered, among others; and group discussions were held, with appropriate permutations of staff taking part, on the issue of whether such psychological 'explanations' were really damaging to Christian belief.

Pupils who were not directly involved in the production of *Dr Faustus* presented, in assembly, extracts from other plays on connected themes, including Sartre's *Huis Clos* and early morality and miracle plays. In art, many pupils who had saturated themselves in Catholic ceremonies and texts attempted a large scale mural depicting hell, and since this was on the wall at the back of the apron stage it became an integral part of the production of Dr Faustus.

'*What do devils look like?*'

This experiment was, I believe, highly successful, though as with any opportunistic educational process it is not easy to give a clear account of *why* it was successful. However, some points are fairly obvious:

(*a*) The interest of most pupils arose spontaneously from an apparently simple but dramatic question: what do devils look like? Why the almost inevitable component of animalism?

(*b*) The staff were not trying to push a particular point of view: there was an atmosphere of genuine enquiry which affected both pupils and teachers.

(*c*) The 'integration' between various subjects arose quite naturally: it was not the sort of tired and woolly integration where several teachers are saying 'Oh God, what can I do about "The Sea" this week?'

(*d*) The intellectual issues (such as 'freedom of will') were ones that could be debated at various intellectual levels, so that while the least able pupils could be involved satisfactorily, the brightest were really being stretched.

3. GROUP DISCUSSION

Admittedly there are not many schools where the *Dr Faustus* episode would have worked out so well. All too often RE is conducted in barren isolation by teachers who resent having to do it at all. For those teachers who find themselves lumbered with two periods a week and wonder what on earth they can do, I should think that guided discussion of the sort I described on pages 59-63 would be quite a useful device, though it would involve going to the trouble of preparing enough topic cards (with theme and a battery of questions).

To end this chapter here is one example of what such cards could look like:

The average man can live a good life
without religion

Would you agree with any of these statements?

(*a*) A man can live a good life without being a Christian and without ever going to church.

(*b*) The average man can live a good life without believing in any kind of god.

(*c*)   *Some* men can live a good life without religion, but *most* men need a religion.

(*d*)   A man can live a good life without religion, *if* he has a strong character and a real love for all humanity.

(*e*)   The average man can live a *fairly* good life without religion, because he is governed to a great extent by the law and by public opinion. But few people lead an *entirely* good life without religion.

(*f*)   Education is more important than religion when it comes to leading a good life.

If you agree with (*c*), (*d*) or (*e*) can you also accept the original statement? What does 'living a good life' mean? Does it just mean *not* breaking the law, *not* outraging public opinion, and *not* treating other people badly? Or does it involve *going out of your way* to help others, treating all people (even enemies) just as you would like *them* to treat you, and if necessary putting the welfare of other people before your own?

Many people lead good lives in the latter sense without being religious, but could the *average* man do so?

Does the average person *want* to be good in this sense, or is it too much like hard work?

What do you think about the following statement?

'No man lives without religion. Even if one is an atheist one lives in a country where standards of behaviour have been created by the impact of religion, and one's character is bound to be influenced, if only indirectly, by religious teaching.'

If a person does not belong to a particular religion, and does not believe in a god or a 'supreme being', is it possible for him to be religious in another sense? Can he have a sort of *faith* in the importance of human dignity, freedom, and equality, and call this a *religion*?

Some opinions to consider

Here are some comments by teenagers in a secondary modern school:

(*a*)   I disagree. If a man thinks there is nothing above him (except kings, queens, etc.) sooner or later he will be tempted to do bad things.

(*b*)   I think that you can live a good life without religion because religion doesn't make you any different.

(*c*)   The *average* man can live a good life without religion. His concern should be his family, his job and his leisure. Religion is a hobby, if you like it you join in.

(*d*)   I agree, because I think that if you didn't think about religion it would not bother you. Many average men do not go to church but they do not suffer.

(*e*)   At least once in their life people must pray to God for some reason or other.

(*f*)   If a man has no religion he has no conscience and doesn't believe in anything except getting a good time out of life.

(*g*)   Most men live a good life and do not go to church but this does not mean they live without religion.

(*h*)   Religion is always out of date on what's good and what's wrong, like with the Pope and the birth pill.

And here are some comments from teachers:

(*a*)   People without religion are 'good' in much the same way that animals are 'good' - obeying their instincts and following the herd.

(*b*)   Religion is not a kind of crutch; it does not provide an easy way of deciding what is right and wrong. But it does *inspire* people to act in the best interest of mankind as a whole. Most people lead selfish, narrow lives, but are less likely to do so if they are religious.

(*c*)   People *should* be able to lead good lives without superstitious beliefs in God and Heaven. In practice, though, religious beliefs have resulted in much better standards of behaviour among uneducated people.

Facts to find

Ask your headmaster if you can invite a *humanist* to talk to your group about his beliefs. The British Humanist Association, 13 Prince of Wales Terrace, London, W.8, would suggest a suitable speaker. Write to the Press and Publications Officer.

St Augustine gave the advice 'Love God, and do what you like'. What did he mean?

What famous people in the past have outraged the public with their views on behaviour, yet are now believed to have been *right* in doing what they did?

Ask teachers to help you find out what these people would probably say about the statement in question: Bertrand Russell, A. J. Ayer, the Bishop of Southwark.

Read *Till We Have Faces* by C. S. Lewis.

Ask your R.I. teacher to explain the importance of the Sermon on the Mount.

What other teenagers think

The average man can live a good life without religion.

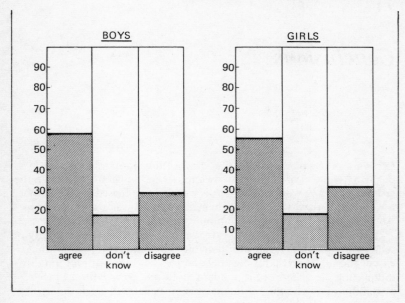

11

Conclusions

Certain teachers who read the first draft of this book told me that I ought to 'come clean' about my own moral and religious beliefs, on the grounds that any work of this sort is bound to be biased by the author's own point of view. (Some of them guessed that I was a soul-searching Anglican, others that I was a communistic atheist.)

Well, I shall come clean, but only because any teacher of morality or religion in schools is faced with precisely the same problem. To what extent should he reveal his own beliefs? Can he do so without unfairly influencing the beliefs of his pupils? Can he *not* do so without the possibility of *more subtly* influencing their beliefs (through the partial presentation of evidence, or through swaying the balance of a discussion - things which can easily happen even if one is consciously on one's guard against them)?

My own feeling is that pupils should always be made aware of the teacher's beliefs in any situation where informal discussions are being used as a teaching process. At its best, education is *conversational*; and as in any other good conversation everyone taking part should be able to learn from everyone else. The teacher's own moral and religious experience is part of what he has to offer, and conversely he should be willing to learn from that of his pupils. However, being more experienced and knowledgeable about subjects in which he has specialised, he should also have the ability to guide the learning processes of the pupils. These two roles, sharer of experience and guide, overlap; both must be conducted with scrupulous honesty. It is easy enough to 'make' pupils, superficially, hold certain intellectual views; it is vastly harder to help them towards forming significant views of their own.

The religious experience that I had to share with my pupils was rather limited. I attended a Church of England primary school where so many (boring) services were held that my mind closed to them before I was eight years old, and remained closed throughout all the routine Bible study which constituted RE in my secondary school.

Consequently (as far as I can remember) I missed the 'authoritarian' and the 'conforming' stages altogether.

At fifteen I encountered the works of Bernard Shaw for the first time, and at once became an 'evolutionist' - a believer in the *élan vital*, or Life Force. The Life Force is that which, at first blind and blundering, forged life out of matter and then slowly promoted the evolution of life forms towards greater intelligence and autonomy. With the creation of Man it became possible for the Life Force to become more effective; for the intelligence of Man became, as it were, the eyes of the Life Force. Man could now 'plug in' to the vast energy of the Life Force and come to control his own destiny. What is morally right is that which promotes the evolution of Man to greater intelligence, to longevity, to complete autonomy. He who fights in the cause can draw strength from the powerful tide of life: he who fights against it has no such resource and, like the dinosaurs, will become extinct. During my adolescence the religion of the Life Force was everything that I needed to make sense of the universe. If the Life Force was the equivalent of a god it was also a god *within oneself*. Bernard Shaw (and, later in my reading, Bergson) were the high priests, or the equivalent of Christ in Christianity. My worship took the form of writing terrible poetry about evolution, and as a disciple I also went out and 'taught' my suffering friends. Most of all, this religion was by no means just 'in the head': it gave me an exhilarating, dynamic sense of purpose in life; it *sang* within me like the hymn 'Jerusalem'.

However, by the age of twenty-one I thought that Bergson was a pretentious mystagogue, Bernard Shaw an arid bore, and the doctrine of the Life Force a rag-bag of dangerous metaphysical nonsense. This was not simply because I had *changed*. I had read more widely, thought more deeply, and now saw that the 'Life Force' was just as unscientific a concept as other deities, and furthermore that 'evolution' or 'progress' are not just the same as 'change'. 'Progress', at least, implies *change for the better*, and if one wanted to judge certain kinds of change to be good then one had to have criteria *other* than the actual change itself whereby to decide that it was change for the *better*. The doctrine of evolution was just one example of fallacious 'descriptive' theories of morality. With this and many other sorts of consideration I slowly demolished my religion. Perhaps there were physical factors as well; it is easier in adolescence to channel one's libido into the fierce holding of spiritual beliefs. Sexual maturity brings different outlets and (sometimes) a more realistic understanding of the world. Small wonder that priests have been the victims of anti-sexual cults.

Rid of what I now regarded as a false religion I was free to move in other directions, but in one mysterious sense a sort of internal light had gone out for good. I have never been 'religious' since, unless a sort of generalised love of people can be called a religion. The rather lurid light of evolutionism has been replaced by a quieter 'faith' in common sense, reason and love.

At twenty-two I had what must be the unusual experience (in this country) of coming to a study of Christianity with completely fresh eyes. I read the Bible for the first time, and many standard religious books. Later I spent a good deal of time talking with Christians for whom I had immense respect and who patiently tried to explain to me exactly what they believed.

To be honest, I still do not understand Christianity. I can appreciate Christ as a moral revolutionary, as a stern, uncompromising teacher. What baffles me is the vast edifice of theology and metaphysics which has been built on such slight foundations. I am also baffled that whenever I point to a feature of Christianity which I regard as categorically Christian (as distinct from features which can also be found in humanism), sophisticated Christians always seem to dismiss them as not very significant. They disagree among themselves about what they mean by 'God'; some say that they wish the word 'soul' had never been invented; many say that concepts such as the Virgin Birth, or the transubstantiation of the bread and wine, are a sort of (important) mythology - and yet do not care about the fact that they are taught as the literal truth. However, I shall continue my education in the hope of gaining better understanding, though at present I am inclined to believe that 'Church Going' by Philip Larkin is a true forecast of the future of religion.

I hope that this autobiographical chapter will not be regarded as mere self-indulgence. In fact it indirectly poses a question which must be faced by all RE teachers.

On the basis of the information I have given, at what stage in my life (if any) would I have best been able to provide religious education in the sense defined in this book? (I do *not* mean any form of evangelism or any sort of attempt to *convert* people to a way of thinking.) During my religious phase, when I was full of enthusiasm for my beliefs (but when I was deaf to other voices)? During my sceptical phase, when I saw the faults as well as the virtues of my religion (but when I was heavily sceptical and disillusioned)? Or during my current non-religious phase, when I am fairly dispassionate and open-minded (but not 'fired' by any really religious belief)?

I hope that you will feel this to be a difficult question, and will consider your own experiences in relation to your role as an educator.

I hope too that you will decide that children, as soon as they are old enough to think for themselves, should encounter teachers who are committed to different faiths (variety is particularly important, perhaps, in multi-racial schools) as well as those who are interested in religion but not committed to any faith themselves. I would also add that in my view they should meet teachers who are both well-informed about, and hostile to, religion.

Suggestions for Further Reading

The following suggestions are listed as being of relevance to particular chapters of this book.

Chapters 1, 2 and 3

1. John Wilson, *Education in Religion and the Emotions* (Heinemann, 1971).
   This is not an easy book and its construction is sometimes confusing. However, I strongly recommend it as a more rigorous presentation of points made in Chapters 1, 2, 3 and 8.

2. R. S. Peters, *The Concept of Motivation* (Routledge, 1960).
   Many relevant points relating analysis of the emotions to the role of the educator.

3. L. Wittgenstein, *Lectures and Conversations* (Blackwell, 1966).
   For serious students of the philosophy of religion and of the emotions.

Chapter 4

1. John Wilson, *Philosophy* (Heinemann, 1969).

2. John Wilson, *Moral Thinking* (Heinemann, 1970).
   Very simple and short introductions to the nature of modern philosophy and to the application of philosophical techniques to moral problems.

3. Mary Warnock, *Ethics since 1900* (OUP, 1960).
   A broader picture of the development of various schools of thought in moral philosophy.

4. R. M. Hare, *Freedom and Reason* (OUP, 1965).
   A comprehensive analysis of the concepts of prescriptivity and universalisability. One of the most important books on moral philosophy to be produced this century.

5. Philippa Foot (ed.), *Theories of Ethics* (OUP, 1967).
   For the serious student of philosophy. A rigorous look at current
   disputes.

Chapters 5 and 6

1. J. Wilson, B. Sugarman and N. Williams, *An Introduction to Moral
   Education* (Penguin, 1968).
   An interdisciplinary study of the concepts and practice of moral
   education. Essential reading for anyone who wishes to have a sound
   theoretical basis in this area.

2. R. S. Peters, *Ethics and Education* (Allen & Unwin, 1966).
   A coherent analysis of the relevance for educational practitioners
   of the work of moral philosophers. Better on theory than practice,
   but this is an extremely important book.

Chapter 8

1. Basil Mitchell (ed.), *Faith and Logic* (Allen & Unwin, 1957).

2. Karl Britton, *Philosophy and the Meaning of Life* (CUP, 1969).

3. Renford Bambrough, *Reason, Truth and God* (Methuen, 1969).

4. D. Z. Phillips (ed.), *Religion and Understanding* (Blackwell, 1967).

   All of these books are fairly readable, and good examples of writings
   which relate modern philosophical thinking to religious concepts.

Chapter 9

1. E. Cox, *Changing Aims in Religious Education* (Routledge, 1966).

2. H. Loukes, *New Ground in Religious Education* (SCM, 1965).

   I have found these two books to contain more clear good sense on
   the subject than any others I have encountered.

Miscellaneous

1. Alan Harris, *Thinking about Education* (Heinemann, 1970).
   A very short and elementary introduction to the philosophy of
   education, with chapters on moral and religious education.

2. Barry Sugarman, *The School and Moral Development* (Croom Helm,
   1973).
   A sociological approach to the role of the school as an instrument of
   'indirect' moral education.

3. N. and S. Williams, *The Moral Development of Children* (Macmillan, 1970).
   An unusually lucid and readable account of the psychology of moral growth.

4. *The Journal of Moral Education*
   This is published quarterly by Pemberton and contains articles concerning both the theory and practice of moral education.